T0316547

Cambridge Elements ☰

Elements in Global Urban History
edited by
Michael Goebel
Graduate Institute Geneva
Tracy Neumann
Wayne State University
Joseph Ben Prestel
Freie Universität Berlin

HOW CITIES MATTER

Richard Harris
McMaster University, Ontario

CAMBRIDGE
UNIVERSITY PRESS

CAMBRIDGE
UNIVERSITY PRESS

University Printing House, Cambridge CB2 8BS, United Kingdom

One Liberty Plaza, 20th Floor, New York, NY 10006, USA

477 Williamstown Road, Port Melbourne, VIC 3207, Australia

314–321, 3rd Floor, Plot 3, Splendor Forum, Jasola District Centre, New Delhi – 110025, India

103 Penang Road, #05–06/07, Visioncrest Commercial, Singapore 238467

Cambridge University Press is part of the University of Cambridge.

It furthers the University's mission by disseminating knowledge in the pursuit of education, learning, and research at the highest international levels of excellence.

www.cambridge.org
Information on this title: www.cambridge.org/9781108749268
DOI: 10.1017/9781108782432

First published 2021

A catalogue record for this publication is available from the British Library.

ISBN 978-1-108-74926-8 Paperback
ISSN 2632-3206 (online)
ISSN 2632-3192 (print)

How Cities Matter

Elements in Global Urban History

DOI: 10.1017/9781108782432
First published online: June 2021

Richard Harris
McMaster University, Ontario

Author for correspondence: Richard Harris, harrisr@mcmaster.ca

Abstract: Most historians and social scientists treat cities as mere settings. In fact, urban places shape our experience. There, daily life has a faster, artificial rhythm and, for good and ill, people and agencies affect each other through externalities (uncompensated effects) whose impact is inherently geographical. In economic terms, urban concentration enables efficiency and promotes innovation while raising the costs of land, housing, and labour. Socially, it can alienate or provide anonymity, while fostering new forms of community. It creates congestion and pollution, posing challenges for governance. Some effects extend beyond urban borders, creating cultural change. The character of cities varies by country and world region, but it has generic qualities, a claim best tested by comparing places that are most different. These qualities intertwine, creating built environments that endure. To fully comprehend such path dependency, we need to develop a synthetic vision that is historically and geographically informed.

Keywords: anonymity, cities, community, comparison, efficiency, externalities, governance, innovation, path dependency, urban networks

ISSNs: 9781108749268 (PB), 9781108782432 (OC)
ISSNs: 2632-3206 (online), 2632-3192 (print)

Contents

1 Introduction

[E]everybody knows what a city is, except the experts.

Horace Miner (1967: 279)

I was sitting in Peter Goheen's graduate seminar on urban historical geography when it happened. He had just introduced the idea that only some of the things that happen *in* cities are truly urban, that is, caused wholly or in part by their urban setting. Doubtless, some of my peers shrugged and began to think of lunch. But for me it marked the slow dawn of a revelation.

I soon discovered that many writers had dismissed this suggestion as being unfounded. Some said that what appears to be the significance of cities – a word I will often use to denote urban places in general – is in fact the product of other forces, commonly the dynamics of capitalism. Others conceded cities might matter but in different ways, in different places, making generalization impossible. And many others reckoned that at one time, perhaps when cities had walls, they might have counted but that that is no longer true. In time, the issue resolved into a question. Apart from the forces that create and work within them, do cities still matter? Put that way, the question answered itself. Of course! Why else would they exist? Why would people cluster together unless they perceived some advantage? And what can we call that advantage other than 'urban'? The relevant question was no longer whether but how cities matter. This Element is my answer.

As you can tell, I became a believer. I address myself to those who are curious about the truth but above all to those like my younger self who have not yet asked the right question. At one point, trudging home at dusk through the first snowfall of a Canadian winter, I reflected that this Element could turn into a useful but dull bibliographic survey. After all, there is a lot of ground to cover and, as recent surveys and encyclopedias have shown, there is a superabundance of published material on the history of cities (Daunton 2000; Clark 2013; Ewen 2016; Gilfoyle 2019); and so I have tried to make it engaging enough to encourage skeptics to keep turning the (paper or digital) pages.

Yet why should we care how cities matter? What difference does it make to how we understand our daily lives or, for those of us who are academics, to what we research and how we teach? For the urbanists, and particularly the urban historians who are my first audience, there is surely the matter of intellectual satisfaction. Having an answer to what Manuel Castells (1977) called 'the urban question' grounds our scholarly identity, explains our engagement with 'urban' organizations, our decision to examine cities and to publish in 'urban' journals. Beyond such professional considerations there is the more public argument that, if cities matter, then to understand the world it behooves us to figure out how.

We owe it to . . . to whom? There are many answers. The most general is "any urban resident who is interested in understanding the places in which they live," and I hope that this Element will appeal to them, too. A more specific audience consists of those who manage and plan cities. Given my own interests, I think of those who wrestle with the challenges of affordable housing. Some argue that residents need higher incomes or easier credit; others that builders must become more efficient, that municipalities should cut red tape, or that homeowners should accept higher-density development. All of these can have merit, but none get at the root of the problem, the high cost of urban land, which arises from the way modern urban housing and land markets work. Among other things, this Element explains what that means.

What We Are Talking About

So what are these things called 'cities' or, more generally, 'urban places'? The best place to start is somewhere simple: agglomerations of people. This basic formula has satisfied notable urbanists such as Bob Beauregard (2018: 5–15), economic historians like Eric Lampard (1961: 56), and the geographers Allen Scott and Michael Storper (2015). People can cram themselves into smaller and smaller spaces, and that is part of the story of cities, above all for the poor. But this also means a denser built environment: homes built side by side, back to back, or on top of one another. Size and density have other correlates and consequences that are so inevitable that they could be counted as part of the very definition of cities. At any rate, they frame and influence each of the major dimensions of urban life discussed in what follows: the economic (Section 3), the social and cultural (Section 4), and the role of governance (Section 5).

To size and density, the most famous urbanist, Louis Wirth ([1938] 1969), added 'heterogeneity'. The linkage comes through the ease and frequency of face-to-face connections in work and public environments. As noted in Section 3, cities support a more elaborate division of labour than dispersed settlements can, so occupational specialization proliferates; they also attract rural and long-distance migrants with different lifeways, languages, and beliefs. And, as discussed in Section 4, cities foster minority lifestyles and associations that deviate from prevailing norms. In other words, it is plausible to think of social diversity as a defining, 'urban' quality. But then so are some other features that Wirth overlooked or downplayed. As discussed in Section 5, and as many have argued, the juxtaposition of people and activities creates challenges which public agencies – typically, municipal governments – have to deal with: noise, water provision, waste disposal, congestion, and the like. Such problems are generic, neither modern nor geographically specific. Two millennia ago, to make traffic manageable the rulers of Pompeii devised a system of one-way streets (Vanderbilt 2008: 8), while Roman cities in general were famed for their efforts to deliver drinking water. Collective provision and governance, then, are surely a defining feature of cities.

So, too, is a distinctive rhythm of life. The lives of urban residents are governed weakly by the seasons, while developments in lighting technology have enabled them to be active at night, whether in shift work or for recreation. In Britain, by the eighteenth century there was an urban 'night life' that threw rural living into the shade (Corfield 1982: 169). Indeed, social proximity encourages night-time activity even without much artificial light. In September 1980, my wife and I arrived at 10 p.m. at the train station in Tianjin, China, then a city of 9 million. Stepping outside we encountered a ghostly flock of cyclists, none with lamps, navigating unlit streets past mostly dark buildings. Where there was a need, or a desire, there was clearly a way.

Rhythm involves timing and pace. If urban life is less governed by the sun it eventually, and increasingly, became regulated by the clock. This was no accident. As David Landes (1983: 71–2) observes, "the city needed to know the time even before the mechanical clock was invented ... necessity was the mother of invention." The first places to acquire public clocks were cities; clocks and their offspring, the wristwatch, gained authority when they became reliable in the early 1800s (McCrossen 2013: 18). In the United States, as the century progressed, the proportion of city people with watches varied with city size and by the 1890s exceeded 50 per cent (McCrossen 2013: 88). At about that time in Berlin, the sociologist Georg Simmel ([1903] 1969: 50) claimed there was a "universal diffusion of pocket watches," for without "strict punctuality ... the technique of metropolitan life is unimaginable."

The precise measurement of time encouraged a faster pace. Simmel ([1903] 1969: 48) reckoned that cities had a "faster rhythm of life" than towns and villages. That contrast still exists. New York's sidewalks are notorious for their head-down hustle, while a survey found that walking speed is correlated with city size, "regardless of cultural setting" (Bornstein and Bornstein 1976: 558). People talk about a 'New York minute', not its Schenectady equivalent. From a field survey that included rural settlements, Paul Amato (1983) found the same contrast in Papua New Guinea. The way pedestrians behave is symptomatic. Another survey found that "after economic well-being, the single strongest predictor of ... tempo ... is population size" (Levine 1997: 16). And, as cities grew larger, ever more ingenious methods were devised to help people to hurry, exploit light, and incidentally make noise (e.g. Mackintosh et al. 2018).

Of course, neither clocks nor a faster pace were due entirely to the size and density of settlement. It was indeed 'the city' that needed to know the time, in order to coordinate people in a division of labour that did not rely on the weather. But what helped drive and perfect the emerging rhythm was the opportunity to make money. As Landes (1983: 91) also observes, it was merchants who "understood that time was money"; he quotes an Italian entrepreneur who in 1433 declared (presumably in Italian), "I'd rather lose sleep than time." By the nineteenth century, what had mattered to merchants became vital to manufacturers who paid by the hour; and so it is that, down to the global urban present, the bundle of money, time, and space that David Harvey (1985) detects in the modern city has become ever tighter. It is only small Norwegian islands that can hope to 'abolish time' (Henley 2019).

Anticipating objections, and issues touched on in Section 5, I must immediately make four things clear. The first is that, mostly, cities do not matter in the way that people or organizations do (Lewis 2017). True, municipal governments make decisions that have consequences, but for the most part urban places matter because of how the agents of history – companies, politicians, interest groups, innovators, and so forth – are juxtaposed. Second, the intensity of urbanism varies and may be increasing. Residential densities may have fallen from their historical peaks in many urban areas, but metropolitan areas are larger than ever and arguably faster and more relentlessly paced now that work and life can proceed 24/7. Third, as almost all observers agree, we should not obsess over any particular number for size or density; it is more helpful to think in terms of a continuum. Fourth, as even Louis Wirth commented, there is no longer a sharp line between urban and non-urban territory. Indeed, since he wrote in 1938, the boundary has become more blurred, to the point that many argue that no such distinction can be made (e.g. Brenner and Schmidt 2014). I disagree and explain why in Section 2, but clearly, here too, we must talk about degrees along a continuum.

We have come some distance from the idea of urban places being defined by size and density. In addition to social heterogeneity, the intrinsic qualities of urban living include collective problems of governance, coupled with a faster, artificial rhythm to life that has been encouraged by the development of merchant, industrial, and now finance capitalism. Researchers and statistical agencies rarely invoke these features when they define cities but, together, they make up a plausible package, 'urbanism'.

Parts and Wholes

Planners and their political bosses cannot afford to ignore any aspect of this package for very long. If they do, residents, commuters, and business people, individually or collectively, will bring neglected concerns to their attention.

Academics are another matter. Except for some brave souls who advise governments, scholars tend to concentrate on one or other aspect of the urban scene. When sociologists, and some anthropologists, speak about urbanism what they have in mind is community life beyond the workplace. Those who study the economy focus on markets and industries, deploying a language of bid rent curves, agglomeration economies, and negative externalities; and political scientists think about interest groups, growth coalitions, and the like. As a result, each discipline often allows the interdependent complexity of the city to slip from view.

Such specialization is a problem if we want to understand historical patterns or trends, which typically have complex causes: the unusual inventiveness of both industry and municipal government in Birmingham, England, in the second half of the nineteenth century; the peculiar role of women in Paris, Ontario, for much of the twentieth; or the strange force of labour strife in Mombasa in the 1940s. It also matters if we want to figure out whether and how cities are distinctive. Some of the strongest challenges to this idea have come from sociologists (e.g. Martindale 1958; Gans 1972; Castells 1976). One, Peter Saunders (1981), wrote a book on the subject, concluding that the urban way of life was simply the result of capitalist-style competition. Even on its own terms, his argument is open to debate (Section 4); but, more to the present point, and like many others, he ignored the dynamics of industry and the challenges of governance. Empirically and conceptually, a partial view can produce a misleading conclusion.

In principle, geographers and historians are more disposed to embrace complexity. To make sense of the way cities are laid out, they take account of all types of spaces, whether homes or workplaces, roads, or other infrastructure, and how people connect such sites on a daily basis. Similarly, to comprehend the character and dynamics of any city over time, they must figure out the changing interplay of all major elements of the local scene. Sometimes geographers have learned from historians, as happened in the 1970s and 1980s, while the subsequent 'spatial turn' has partially reversed the direction of influence (Gunn 2001). Unfortunately, both have also specialized – by topic, city, nation, or all three. Leading scholars have regularly noted and regretted this sub-specialization (Stave 1983: 417). In 1973, Jim Dyos ([1973] 1982a: 35) worried that the "vast outpouring of writings" described "countless, minuscule, urban-centred happenings" that were "a challenge to the digestion, not the head," echoing E. H. Carr's (1964: 15) earlier complaint about the trend of "historians knowing more and more about less and less." How much truer today! And then, across all disciplines, the case study dominates. Researchers focus on particular themes in single cities, not the broader, collective significance of urbanization

(Hays 1993; but see Lampard 1983; Bairoch 1988). It becomes easy to lose sight of the significance of the urban and wider whole. If there is one thing that this Element tries to do it is to encourage and enable people to see the importance of a bigger, indeed global, urban picture.

Places and Times

Global but not historically comprehensive. A few writers have followed Lewis Mumford's (1961) example of surveying cities throughout history, but this Element focuses only on cities since the rise of industrial capitalism from the late eighteenth century. The reasoning is that the rise of the industrial, as opposed to mercantile, form of capitalism transformed the character of cities, stimulating their growth to an unprecedented size. More importantly, it enabled urbanization – a growing *proportion* of people living in cities – on a transformative scale (Weber [1899] 1963). In the process, it brought successive waves of globalization, initially through the trading networks of European powers, that transplanted versions of capitalism to almost every urban place. I happen to believe that many of the arguments discussed here are relevant to pre-industrial cities but, except for passing references, I am sensible enough to make no such claim.

For most of the past two centuries, globalization increased the contrasts in wealth between what came to be known, after 1945, as the developed and developing worlds, reframed more recently as the global North and South. In recent decades, however, an increasing number of countries, including Japan, South Korea, Turkey, and above all China, have blurred and crossed that conceptual divide. At the same time, the relevance to the South of "parochial" concepts and assumptions developed by Northern theorists has been questioned (Robinson 2011: 10). This does not mean that we should abandon attempts to develop an understanding of the urban question that are applicable everywhere. Indeed, this Element argues that such a goal is feasible and important. But it does mean that Northerners should not take things for granted and be open to the idea that concepts developed in, or hitherto seen as uniquely relevant to, the South might be as relevant to Kingston, Ontario, as they are to Kingston, Jamaica. A notable example is the concept of informality, that is, economic activity that contravenes regulations and/or evades taxes (Portes and Haller 2005). As Jenny Robinson (2005) has argued, for certain purposes we should think of cities everywhere as essentially the same, 'ordinary'.

The Campaign Plan

If cities are complex wholes, why are the core sections of this Element organized thematically: economy, then social and cultural life, and finally governance. But what else is possible? Wholes are made of parts, and skipping over the particulars in order to concentrate on the big picture would produce waffly generalities that signified little. What, then, binds the particulars together? Under the label of urbanism, I have already pointed to some general considerations: social heterogeneity, collective challenges, pace, artificial rhythm. Underlying and connecting many of these are externalities, a term favoured by economists. These are the uncompensated, non-market effects that we have as individuals, and as social or economic organizations, upon one another. They can produce unlooked for benefits as well as costs and resentments. Their impact typically declines, often rapidly, away from their point of origin, and so urban concentrations magnify their effects. These bring social, economic, and political dynamics into a complex interrelation, with unpredictable results.

Here, economy, society, and governance are given roughly equal weight. This does not imply a judgment; we cannot assess their relative importance, given that all three are essential and intertwined. Historians and social scientists are both cited liberally throughout, because both have many valuable things to say but not always equally. Historians have said little about the nitty-gritty of the urban economy. This is unfortunate because this is one area where there are good reasons to believe that 'path dependence' – a.k.a. the importance of history – is a key to success (or failure). So Section 3 relies on the work of economists and economic geographers, introducing concepts with which some urban historians will be unfamiliar. In contrast, historians have had plenty to say about the sociocultural and political aspects of city life. Because the former remains controversial and subject to misunderstanding, Section 4 clarifies concepts and debates. In contrast, the role of governance is clearer and better documented. Although Section 5 is framed in terms of a conception of the urban land nexus little used by historians, for many readers its account may be the most familiar part of this Element.

Cities, then, shape the lives of their residents, but it is the effects they have beyond their geographical limits which put the seal on their significance. Section 6 opens by sketching the types of connections that carry the influence of cities to other urban centres and to the wider world. It then turns to consider the way in which we, as researchers, need to look beyond any single city's limits in order to test whether the sorts of general claims made here can stand up. In particular, and in light of the suggestion that cities everywhere have features in common, it argues that we should devote more energy to comparing places that, on the face of it, are as different as, well, the two Kingstons.

All of these are arguments that could most effectively be made in different ways to different people. Each discipline has its own biases. Economists need little persuasion about the value of comparative research; sociologists and anthropologists are more likely to prioritize a deep dive into local communities. Yet the greatest and most general contrast is that which exists between social scientists and historians. One emphasizes the importance of developing and testing 'theory'; the other uses it sparingly, if at all. Now, although I am leery of the term 'theory', in part because it can sound pretentious to some, it is clear that the present Element addresses a general question with conceptual aspects. Because it is one of a series that are directed primarily at urban historians, I believe it is useful, and perhaps necessary, to make the case for theory. That is the thankless task of the next section.

2 Historians and the Urban Question

[A] little bit of theory goes a long way.

Reinhard Bendix (cited in Stinchcombe 1968)

Scholars will probably always contest the meaning of 'urban' and 'city'. By now the debate is pointless ... People identify cities as places; what happens in those places is considered 'urban'.

Tim Gilfoyle (1998)

[T]he more sociological history becomes, and the more historical sociology becomes, the better for both.

E. H. Carr (1964)

Reinhard Bendix was advising his colleagues in sociology to tone down their emphasis on theory but, judging by what we write, most urban historians would say he didn't go far enough. We freely use terms like 'race', 'class', 'community', and, of course, 'urban' but, like Tim Gilfoyle, most see little need to engage in conceptual debates. Still, as E. H. Carr implied, that can be a problem.

Where Is the Theory in Urban History?

The reluctance of most urban historians to engage with theory is no different from their colleagues in other subfields of the discipline (Stone 1977: 23; Sewell 2005). For us, it takes the form of a reluctance to deal with the urban question. In his editor's introduction to *Cities in World History*, Peter Clark (2013) skirts the issue, and so does Tim Gilfoyle (2019), editor of the *Oxford Encyclopedia of American Urban History*. Nancy Kwak (2018) raises the possibility of a systematic treatment in her contribution to an interdisciplinary survey, *Defining the Urban*, but opts for a narrative about how urban historians have undertaken their work. Similar reticence is apparent in surveys of a sister subdiscipline, planning history, although land planning is quintessentially an urban issue (e.g. Hein 2018).

This reticence, verging on refusal, is not for want of urgings from a succession of leading Anglo-American scholars. The following is a mere sample. In the 1960s, Eric Lampard (1961: 54) identified the need for a "conceptual framework" while Jim Dyos ([1973] 1982b: 63) asked his colleagues to reflect on how "the experience of living in towns differed, if at all, from the country" and to consider whether "such differences are those of quality rather than degree." In the 1970s, the historical geographer Peter Goheen (1974: 369) observed that the urban question had been lost in empirical detail, and soon Theodore Hershberg (1981: 3) re-emphasized the need to distinguish between the roles of the city as a dependent and an independent variable. Complaints persisted through the 1980s and 1990s (Jansen 1996). Eric Monkkonen (1988) deplored the way urban historians treated cities only as a stage, failing to consider what 'urban' means, and why it mattered, while Richard Rodger (1993: 4) noted, not for the first time, "the absence of theory in urban history." The new millennium brought no rest. In Britain, Rodger (2003: 60) again, and with Roey Sweet (Rodger and Sweet 2008), worried about the neglect of this 'central issue', as the cultural turn had eroded some of the limited identity that urban history already had. Across the Atlantic, surveying the "state of the art," Clay McShane (2006: 595) noted the paucity of theory in American urban history; and in their introduction to an American reader, Steven Corey and Lisa Boehm (2011: 15) commented that urban historians still resisted theory, flubbing Lampard's repeated challenge. The literatures on the history of Canadian, and for that matter South African, cities have attracted similar comments (Stelter 1977; Bickford-Smith 2016: 2–4). The chorus has not let up.

No wonder Sam Bass Warner (1991: 6) once asked (ruefully?) in a presidential address to the Urban History Association, "why are we always preaching at each other?" The answer is clear: many of our leading scholars have believed we should do more than trace what happened at particular places and times. They have wanted us to spend more time ruminating on the core propositions that might define our field.

Such admonitions have always been more relevant in some places than others. English-language historical scholarship is known for its strong "empirical tradition" (Cannadine 1982: 218). Indeed, Cannadine (1982: 204) mischievously suggests that it was only when Jim Dyos came along in the 1960s that British urban historians discovered "what they were doing." Richard Rodger and Roey Sweet (2008) make a further distinction, suggesting that American urban historians have been even less interested in the 'urban question' than the British. That may have been true in recent years but, in the middle decades of the twentieth century, in the hands of Arthur Schlesinger (1933, [1949] 1973), Richard Wade (1959, 1964) and Blake McKelvey (1963) the reverse was true. At any rate, it does seem that French, and other European, writers such as Paul Bairoch (1988) have worked harder to identify generic urban conditions and effects (Rodger 1993: 1; cf. Jansen 1996). For that reason, European surveys generally say more about the significance of cities than those dealing solely with Britain or North America. In *The Making of Urban Europe, 1000–1994*, for example, Paul Hohenberg and Lyn Lees (1995: 248–289) devote a chapter to the human consequences of urbanization. But, to the extent they exist, these national differences are unstable and are only matters of degree. E. H. Carr would probably reckon that they could all do with a bigger dose of theory.

There are signs that the steady growth of urban historical research on the global South is providing something of an exception. The picture is still unclear, in part because the field is so diverse, encompassing much of the world. Certainly, social scientists there have been giving thought to the urban question and, because of the colonial legacy, have paid attention to the urban past (Robinson 2005; Roy 2015). Urban historians, too, have drawn more explicitly on the ideas of social theorists. They draw on political economy (Nieto 2019), poststructuralism (Mayne 2017), and postcolonialism (Alexanderson 2019), broadly cultural interpretations that speak of gendered and racialized identity (Rogaski 2004; Bickford-Smith 2016; Prestel 2017; Banerjee 2019) and sometimes simultaneously (Yeoh 1996; Lewis 2016; Kim 2019; cf. Davis 2005). Dealing, as many have, with colonial eras, they have had to come to terms with large, competing interpretations of historical change. This is perhaps an appropriate place to assert the claim that, just as the broad lines of argument developed in what follows are valid in both the global North and South, they are useful and relevant to any and all of the social theories mentioned here.

Why 'Urban' Theory Matters

Yet if most urban historians have paid little attention to the urban question, why should we care? There are two ways of answering this. One is that theory is embedded in the categories we use and the questions we ask and that it is healthy to be aware of these in order to test our assumptions. Maybe not all the time – that would be exhausting – but at least on a regular basis. That, and its ramifications, comprises the principled line of argument.

There is also pragmatic self-interest, and this may carry more weight. To use a term very popular lately, it is a matter of identity. If 'urban' has no particular significance, why call ourselves urban historians? If we study things that happen in cities, then that is more or less everything ... and nothing special. The immediate result, as flagged by many of the commentators quoted in the previous subsection, is fragmentation, incoherence, and in sum the "lack of [a] canon" (Corey and Boehm 2011: 19). To the extent that that is true, the disparate topics published in our journals and presented at conferences can appear unrelated, with consequences for the quality of dialogue.

The larger practical effect is to question our contribution to the discipline of history and the field of urban studies. Why should historians of labour, business, gender, or race listen to what we have to say if that seems to be nothing special? And what do we have to say to social scientists in urban studies? Currently, social scientists seem to assume the answer is: not much (Beauregard 2004). Examples can be chosen almost at random. In 1986, Peter Goheen reported that "signs of a continuing disregard of the value of historical inquiry linger in the writings of urban geography" (Goheen 1986: 258). Two decades on, Phil Hubbard (2006) surveyed the ways in which various disciplines viewed cities, not including history. Five years later, the editors of the *Blackwell Companion to the City* assembled diverse materials but included no serious treatment of history or of historical thinking (Bridge and Watson 2011). At the same time, an exhaustive survey of urban studies, based on citation indexes, identified seven subfields: geography, economics, sociology, governance, planning, environmental studies, and, lastly, housing and neighbourhood development (Bowen, Dunn, and Kasdan 2010). History was missing, although many of the works cited were historical in character (Harris and Smith 2011). History is overlooked even when in plain view.

The way to make our presence felt, as E. H. Carr implied, and as others such as Charles Tilly (1996) and Bob Beauregard (2004) have suggested, is to speak some of the language of social science. Lawrence Stone (1977: 19) put this bluntly: "to ignore the contributions of the social sciences is clearly fatal." A first step is for us to show that we can, and often do, think in general terms about cities and urbanization; a second is to articulate what a historical perspective can bring to the table. The first is the main concern of the present work, but it is worth giving a nod to the second. Of course, many writers have made the general case for History. An influential statement was offered by William Sewell (2005: 280), who claims the logic of history has five interrelated aspects: "fatefulness, contingency, complexity, eventfulness, and causal heterogeneity." A general takeaway might be the need for humility when making theoretical claims. A useful caution, but is there something more specific that urban historians might have to say about urban places?

Two answers come to mind. One begins with an insight: complexity, thy name is city. Again and again, writers have shown how urban concentration complicates, heightens, and changes the life and work of residents. Historians relish the "the vast confusion of the modern city" (Warner 1962: vii). We have learned to recognize and handle it, employing a synthetic vision. We supposedly have a sensibility and skills that might be shared with those who prefer to analyze and simplify. A second answer begins with the fact, and idea, of path dependency. For some it is a revelation how much the past weighs on the present, with all that that implies for fatefulness, contingency, and eventfulness. That weight poses problems for those who try to explain current patterns in terms of current processes. But, for those open to historical thinking, attending to the past's legacy offers a rich understanding of the way the world works.

This insight has endless applications, one which some social scientists recognize. Take, for example, students of politics and industrial decline. Joel Rast (2012) shows that the form of urban politics in particular American cities depends on events, and decisions made, decades earlier. At a national scale, Zack Taylor (2014) shows that the divergent paths of local governments in Canada and the United States stem from constitutional powers defined centuries ago. In Italy, Putnam (1993) has argued that long-standing regional differences in civic involvement account for the poverty of the South. Awareness of such trajectories is instinctive for urban historians. For example, Tom Sugrue (1996) shows that to make sense of how Detroit fell apart from the 1960s we need to start decades earlier. We should market this sort of understanding.

The notion of path dependency has also been invoked by those studying urban and regional decline (e.g. Polèse 2009). As Asa Briggs (1968) argued, specialization, exemplified by Manchester, England, can involve short-run gain for long-run pain, as innovation atrophies. In contrast, diversified cities continued to thrive. In the nineteenth century, Birmingham contained many small workshops in metal fabrication and spinning, button- and watchmaking, and jewellery. (Adam Smith's celebrated disquisition on the division of labour, illustrated by the manufacture of pins, was based on observation of a Birmingham workshop.) Small factories, diverse occupations, and cooperation between entrepreneurs and workers fostered innovation and enabled businesses to adapt as markets changed (cf. Scott 2000). The company where my father worked had started by making watch dials in the 1800s but graduated to speedometers and car parts in the 1920s. Detroit and Manchester suffered from path dependence; for decades, Birmingham thrived on it. No one is better fitted to make that case than a historian.

In fact, there is no subfield of history better positioned to make the case for path dependency than the urban. The built environment lasts – the street layout even more than individual buildings: in 2004, much of the Indonesian city of Banda Aceh was obliterated by a tsunami but rebuilding revived the previous layout. Those oblivious to such inertia can make egregious mistakes. Toronto provides a good example (Harris and Lewis 1998). In the 1980s, the city's transit system, which extended into the inner suburbs, was praised for its efficiency and high ridership. Experts flew from Australia and the United States to see what the Toronto Transit Commission (TTC) was doing right. What escaped them was that much credit was due to the inaction of the Toronto Street Railway (TSR), the company that ran the streetcar system until 1921. The TSR had remained profitable by refusing to extend lines into fringe subdivisions – no 'streetcar suburbs' there. As a result, Toronto's walkable interwar suburbs were developed at high densities, making them transit-viable when the TTC later took over the system. To emulate Toronto, other cities would have had to turn their clocks back three-quarters of a century and prohibit transit and automobiles at the urban fringe.

At a larger scale, historical legacies can be even more telling. How commonly do towns, still less cities, fade and disappear? Some small-resource communities become ghosts, as has happened with many of Newfoundland's fishing outports. But, as Paul Hohenberg (2004) emphasizes in his historical geography of European cities, urban places persist and long after their heyday. Locals get by; governments offer relief to residents and incentives to businesses; in time, with luck, fortunes revive, perhaps when someone like Quicken Loans' Dan Gilbert sees the potential of cheap real estate and/or pliant workers. Some reinvent themselves as tourist destinations: think Bruges. From one point of view this is inefficient: investments might more profitably be made elsewhere. For that reason, David Harvey (1985) has argued that the immobility of the urban built environment, as fixed capital, challenges the stability of capitalism. But persistence can make sense: a declining settlement is still home to many, while abandoning buildings and infrastructure is wasteful. Of course, both interpretations can be true. Yet, however judged, the path dependence of the urban built environment is one way in which cities cry out for historical treatment.

Of course, in speaking to urban historians about complexity and path dependence, I am preaching to the converted. The point is that there are many non-believers and that, to convert them, we need to learn something of their language.

Encouraging Notes

In the process, we should not judge ourselves too harshly. The reluctance to consider, abstractly, that urban places might have their own significance is not unique. Almost half a century ago, John Walton and Louis Masotti (1976: 3) deplored the way their social science colleagues gave little thought to what was "distinctively urban," noting that much of what passed for 'urban' research was nothing of the sort. That is still fair comment.

Up to a point, the reluctance of all urbanists to define our subject is understandable. We live in a world where sprawl has blurred boundaries, raising questions about the very identity of cities. Beginning in the United States, then in Europe and with a global chorus joining in, commentators have suggested that urban concentration no longer matters (Webber 1964; Lang 2003; Champion 2007). Inspired by Henri Lefebvre (2003), some have suggested that the whole world is in effect, or in the late stages of becoming, urban (Friedmann 2002; Brenner and Schmidt 2014). Historians are surely alert to such current trends and commentary. This is especially true of those who focus on the twentieth century, including the early postwar decades (McShane 2006). So why fret about the 'urban question' when the city itself seems to be in question?

Historians have hinted that they are aware of this issue. Writing in 1969, Jim Dyos ([1969] 1982: 64) conceded that "the physical artefact of the city is beginning to disintegrate"; a decade later, Gunter Barth (1980: 234), having argued for the emergence of a distinctively urban culture in America in the late 1800s, suggested that the telephone, radio, and car had eroded the importance of propinquity; more recently, introducing an edited survey of the modern history of urban Britain to 1950, Martin Daunton (2000: 53–55) pointed out that the identity of cities is being eroded. The message, echoed and implied by others as well, is that the urban question may be becoming redundant (cf. Handlin 1963: 24; Fraser and Sutcliffe 1983: xxii–xxvii).

I do not believe that. The purpose of the next four sections is to marshal evidence and arguments to support the claim that urban concentration has shaped our economy, society, and collective governance and continues to do so. This has ramifications most obviously for the residents of cities but indeed for people everywhere.

3 The Economic Significance of Cities

The city is many things: it is a cultural focus, a social resort, a political center, but before all – though not above all – it is a place where people earn a living.

Richard Wade (1959: 39)

The concentration of economic resources in large metropolitan centers has brought about the most effective utilization of resources, human and material, yet known to society.

Norman S. B. Gras (1925)

We don't need Richard Wade to tell us that the city's economy is of fundamental importance, although we will have reason to recall his cautionary aside. But in pointing to the importance of agglomeration, Norman Gras begs the questions how and why, questions that urban historians have rarely considered. On this, more than any other subject, we should listen to what others have had to say. This section surveys what is known about how cities promote economic efficiency and innovation, although not always and not necessarily to the benefit of all.

Never let it be said that urban historians have ignored the importance of the city's economy. To be sure, on some occasions North Americans have often been able to take its health for granted. When Arthur Schlesinger (1933; [1949] 1973), the doyen of American urban history, wrote about urban civilization he covered a wide territory but said little about merchants, manufacturers, and financiers. Similarly, surveying the twentieth-century metropolis, Jon Teaford (2006: 3) did not take time to explain the prosperity that has produced an "amorphous sprawl"; and, mea culpa, I have done the same thing myself. But other surveys and case studies have acknowledged the determining influence of the economy on city growth and character. Examples include studies of places as different as London (Dyos and Reeder 1973) and Mombasa (Cooper 1987). Many writers have focused on manufacturing cities, arguing, with Ralph Turner ([1940] 1973), that the rise of industry created a new type of city (Stave 1981). Gideon Sjoberg (1960) elaborated the argument, and historians have studied the local impact of manufacturing. Prominent examples include Maury Klein and Harvey Kantor's (1976) outline of industrial urbanization and accounts of North American cities such as Philadelphia (Hershberg 1981) and Montreal (Lewis 2000); of British cities such as Coventry (Prest 1960); of industrial towns such as Paris and Hanover, Ontario (Parr 1990); and, at a smaller scale, of working-class neighbourhoods (Barrett 1987). The impact of industry has also been acknowledged by those interested in politics and government (e.g. Briggs 1968) or the social geography of cities in Britain (Dennis 1984) and North America (Zunz 1982). And, of course, it has concerned those interested in the effects of deindustrialization, together with attempts to mitigate its effects (Sugrue 1996; Neumann 2016). Clearly, urban historians know that, when it comes to understanding urban growth and change, 'it's the economy, stupid'.

Yet they have rarely reversed the causality and asked how agglomeration has helped firms, industries, and hence the economy as a whole. The exception, of course, is the succession of economists, economic historians, and lately economic geographers, from Alfred Marshall (1922) and Norman Gras (1925), through Edgar Hoover (1948), Bert Hoselitz (1955), and Eric Lampard (1955), to Paul Bairoch (1988), Lionel Frost (1998), Paul Hohenberg (2004), Edward

Glaeser et al. (1992), and Michael Storper (2013). Unfortunately, economic history has struggled. As Alan Beattie (2009: 2, 3) observes, it "involves forcing together disciplines that naturally fall out in different directions," by which he means "narrative" versus "universal rules." The task of bridging this divide has sometimes fallen to economic sociologists. Mark Granovetter (1985: 486), for example, has influentially warned economists against "abstract[ing] away from . . . the historical and structural embeddedness of relations." We will return to one of his examples, the building industry, in "The Housing Market" subsection.

Even given the weakness of economic history, its connections with urban history have been limited, especially in North America (Mohl 1998). When urban history engaged with theory in the 1960s it linked with sociology (Thernstrom 1973; Hershberg 1981). Lately, it has been influenced by the cultural turn (Gilfoyle 1998; Ewen 2016: 24–28). As a result, a recent survey of Urban History Association members revealed many more interested in planning, or the social and political aspects of cities, than in trade, industry, and finance (Harris 2019). Apart from urban journals, members read and publish either in venues with a broad national scope or in those with a planning, environmental, and social focus. These patterns reflect a long-standing gap in our understanding of modern cities.

The Economic Impact of Cities

Filling that gap requires a self-conscious effort but is not an insuperable task. When, in the early 1950s, Lampard (1955) and Hoselitz (1955) framed arguments about the economic significance of cities they were loners. Since the 1960s, however, economists have paid attention to the issues they raised: Paul Krugman (1991) earned a Nobel Prize, partly for work in this area. Today, a body of work demonstrates how concentrations of businesses and skilled workers fuel technological innovation and economic growth.

Of course, this literature must be approached critically. Some writers overstate the point. Jane Jacobs (1969), who has influenced this field as much as she has urban design, sometimes got carried away. Recently, summarizing the favourable accounts, the economist Edward Glaeser (2011) has acted the cheerleader, celebrating *The Triumph of the City* (cf. Brugmann 2009: 24–32). Such boosterism has attracted critics, who remind us that urban concentration has downsides too, including stress, competition, congestion, and concentrations of air and water pollution (Henderson 1988; Tarr 1996; Gleeson 2014). Not all cities foster innovation or enable efficiency, as a glance at modern-day Caracas confirms. Civil strife and natural disasters can cause havoc, as the residents of Homs can testify. Specialization can lead to inflexibility, while rigid control by upper levels of government can stifle technical and entrepreneurial creativity (Polèse 2020). For centuries, Chinese rulers channelled the elite's ambitions into public administration, not production (Murphy 1954; Hung and Zhan 2013). And then, as the recent experience of many cities in the global South shows, massive rural-urban migration can overwhelm the capacity of municipal governments to make their cities work. In part, the existence of extensive shantytowns in many parts of the global South is testimony to what some call 'overurbanization'.

Bearing such points in mind, balanced assessments have been offered by those with a historical perspective. Hoselitz (1955) contrasted 'generative' and 'parasitic' cities, while Beauregard (2018: x) replied to Glaeser's sales job by emphasizing that "the city is the ground on which society's contradictions are contested." The sort of undramatic assessment that Martin Daunton (2000: 48) offered for British cities, 1850–1950, sounds right: "[they] were a complex balance between the diseconomies of pollution and disease, and the economies of information and knowledge." The trick, for any place and time, is to determine what that balance is.

Efficiencies

With cautions noted, what are the potential economic advantages of agglomeration? In terms of magnitude, the consensus is: substantial (Krugman 1991; Rodríguez-Pose and Crescenzi 2008; Storper 2013; Scott and Storper 2015; Rossi 2017). In Section 1, it was suggested that clustering encourages people to compete and live at a faster pace. In modern capitalist cities, one corollary is that people work harder: the rat race is real (Klein and Kantor 1976: 171–174; Rosenthal and Strange 2004: 2143). More generally, Philip McCann (2011: 167) summarizes the prevailing view: "the evidence in favor of the role played by agglomeration economies in promoting growth is now so overwhelming that it is really beyond debate." If cities are insufficient for economic growth they do appear to be necessary.

What, then, are these agglomeration economies? The economist Edgar Hoover (1948: 116–144) identified three types. First, cities help firms reap economies of scale, which Hoover terms 'internal returns to scale' because they stay within factory walls. Employees in larger enterprises are more productive, because size permits a finer division of labour. Only an urban place can provide the necessary workforce, along with family members and ancillary and service workers. Early examples include Glasgow's shipyards (Davies 2019); a recent illustration is Foxconn's operations in Shenzhen. Scale economies extend to transportation (Polèse 2009: 33–49). Bulk freight is key. Railroads and then trucks revolutionized transportation on land while containers have transformed ports (for good and ill) and fostered globalization (Levinson 2006).

For businesses serving a local market, concentrated demand is also a benefit (Glaeser et al. 1992: 1149). A supermarket serving thousands can charge less than a corner store. The same principle affects lawyers, accountants, and engineers, because urban settings support specialized expertise. Population thresholds also matter socially and politically (Granovetter 1978). And they affect economic opportunities, because more specialized services become possible when population thresholds are crossed (Berry and Garrison 1958). The Irish village where I once stopped boasted a combined gas station/store/fast food (sandwiches to order) operation, with a pub attached. Being Ireland, the town ten miles away had several pubs, as well as cafés and a Chinese restaurant. It was cousin to the fictional community of Optimo in the southwestern United States, that J. B. Jackson (1952) once described, with its courthouse, town hall, Ranch Café, movie theatre, and Slymaker's Mercantile clustered around the square. Then, arriving in Dublin, I found countless pubs, Chinese restaurants emphasizing regional and fusion fare, and all the museums, head offices, and institutions of a national capital. Up to a point, such specialization creates greater efficiency. This helps the provider, but competitors too, to the consumer's benefit. As Alan Beattie (2009: 69) observes, "cities are not just the best places to produce services but the best places to consume them."

The other two types of agglomeration economies depend on externalities, that is, effects that extend beyond factory walls and are not monetized (Marshall 1922: 271–273; Bogart 1998). External economies can be positive or negative and, because their effects decline with distance, cities heighten the impact of both. Negative examples include air and water pollution, which challenge governance. But urbanization brings substantial positive externalities too, for employers, employees, and indeed all urban residents. Those created for firms are critical. Unfortunately, only a handful of urban historians have used this concept to explain the significance of urbanization (Morris 1990; Reeder and Rodger 2000: 556–559) or industrial dynamics in a particular city (e.g. Lewis 2008). Externalities lower transaction costs, whether these involve face-to-face communication or the movement of goods.

Easier communication affects both of the other two types of agglomeration effects: 'urbanization' and 'localization' economies (Hoover 1948: 116–144; Henderson 1988). The former are the general advantages of being located in an urban area, such as having access to a large labour pool, to supply chains that provide raw or partially fabricated materials, to transportation facilities, to banking, insurance, and legal services, as well as to public services such as waste disposal and educational and health facilities for employees. Localization economies stem from the particular concentration of companies in the same industry, which use the same supply chains. Educational facilities matter here, too, but in specialized fields. As Andrew and Lynn Lees (2007: 135) note, "knowledge-based industries – engineering, electricity, and chemicals, for example – thrived in cities where schools could train personnel." This encourages a labour pool with specialized skills, and of suppliers and professional services, including marketing, with expertise relevant to the industries in question.

Such concentrations increase competition. This is uncomfortable, but firms commonly benefit more than suffer. There are 'knowledge spillovers', industrial secrets that are transmitted formally, through training, and informally, in convivial social settings – bars, cafés, clubs, all of which can be the result of "semi-conscious and semi-voluntary cooperation" (Becattini 1990: 42, 46; Rosenthal and Strange 2004: 2148–2154). Such 'buzz' depends on face-to-face contact which, as Storper and Venables (2004) argue, is ideal for solving problems, motivating, and fostering trust. These involve what Granovetter (1973) calls the 'weak ties' that link acquaintances, not friends, and are features of the urban scene. Many industries relish such economies, notably Hollywood, whose buzz benefited studios as well as movie-goers everywhere (Scott 2000).

These arguments derive from studies of the global North. Do they apply, or do they have to be adapted, for Southern cities? Until recent decades the question would have been discouraged. Across sub-Saharan Africa, for example in Kenya and South Africa, colonial powers resisted urbanization, thinking Africans to be unsuited for modern life. Indeed, until the 2000s international agencies also questioned rapid urbanization because it caused social and health problems (Bryceson 2014). Lately attitudes have shifted, so that a recent UN global survey emphasized how cities could promote innovation and economic growth (UN Habitat 2013: 123–145). There are indeed some Southern cities with Northern-style industrial districts; Bangalore and Shenzhen are prime examples (Narayana 2011). Even there, however, the question is how informal economic activity affects the situation, because such activity is especially common in the South (Roy 2005; Moreno-Monroy 2012; Harris 2018). It is hard to generalize, because good evidence is scarce and there are different types of informal work. The 'modern' type, linked with formal production, involves suppliers and subcontractors. Its clustering may contribute to industrial efficiency but also the exploitation of workers. Johannesburg provides a well-documented example (Robinson 2005: 162), as does Tiruppur, India, whose growth depended less on the mechanization of the cotton knitwear industry than on long hours for workers, a common pattern (Cawthorne 1995). The more 'traditional' type entails subsistence activity, including street sellers, oriented to local and at most regional markets especially where, as in Kinshasa, road conditions and networks are poor (McCormick 1999; Davies 2019). It typically involves people – commonly women – self-employed and without access to capital (Chant and McIlwaine 2016: 193–198). Survival, not efficiency, is their goal. Some of these arguments surely apply in the global North, too, but the issue has not been explored there. And so, the significance of industrial clustering varies from place to place but especially in the South.

The important scale of concentration has generally grown (Phelps and Ozawa 2003). The greatest benefits of localization have been apparent in tightly defined industrial districts, such as Birmingham's jewellery quarter, or those in Berlin, Singapore, Beijing, Hanoi, and several modern Italian cities (Becattini 1990; Scott 2000; Krätke 2015: 62–70). Chicago's varied districts have been the subject of a particularly fine historical study (Lewis 2008). At a larger scale, 'untraded interdependencies' develop region-wide (Storper 1995). Examples include the electronics industry across the northeastern United States, as well as heavy industries in the Ruhr, the region centred on Pittsburgh, and the Black Country in the English Midlands (Reuleche 1984; Polèse 2009). Most developed spontaneously. As their merits became apparent, however, groups of industrialists and developers planned them. Eventually, municipalities and governments designated special economic zones. These have become popular, notably in China, and most spectacularly in Shenzhen (Du 2020). The city, as we normally define it, is not the only scale at which concentration helps industry.

The Housing Market

As firms congregate, indirectly they create another benefit. If a firm locates in a rural area or small town, it may have difficulty recruiting labour. For year-round work, landowners often provided tenant farmers with 'tied cottages' or, in the American south until the 1860s, slave quarters, while company towns included company housing (Green 2019). That is an added expense and creates a dilemma during downturns. The employer-landlord has three options: employ workers to do nothing; forego or lower rents; or evict those who cannot pay. None are appealing, and making the wrong choice can be disastrous, as George Pullman discovered in his company town during the downturn of the 1890s (Buder 1967). For the employer, then, an advantage of the city is being relieved of having to think about housing. Eventually, the separation of work and home transferred the responsibility for housing workers, with social and political consequences discussed in later sections.

This development was probable, not inevitable. For a time, Chinese cities provided an exception. From the 1930s until recently, state-owned businesses in effect operated company towns within larger urban settings: employees in *danwei* factories were housed next door, and the company provided community and recreational facilities (Bray 2005). This exception does not contradict the rule. Wholesale control over workers' lives was inefficient and enabled resistance (Hsing 2010: 219–220). As the Chinese government withdrew from state-owned operations, *danwei* units broke up, markets for land and labour have emerged, new types of social control have been exerted, and urban economies have boomed (Wu and Gaubatz 2013). The logic of the urban setting is to encourage a separation of work and home.

This arrangement has many consequences. It has usually benefited workers, who are no longer subject to close control: Pullman prohibited saloons in his town. In the city, once workers left the factory or the office, their lives were their own, although sometimes (as with Henry Ford) employers tried to extend supervision into the home (Barrow 2015: 119–123). But here, too, there may not be a net benefit. There is no guarantee that workers will find affordable, decent housing. Historically, slum housing was the main concern, as it still is in the global South (Mayne 2017). Today in the North, the issue is affordability. Occasionally, as in Seattle, major employers offer to subsidize affordable housing, but these are the exception. Urban settings encourage employers to leave an orphaned housing problem at the door of the market or the state.

The emergence of an autonomous housing market may be the greatest consequence of the separation of home and work. The social and political aspects are considered in the next two sections. Geographically, it enabled a growing physical split (Vance 1967). Exclusively residential areas grew up, enabled by new methods of transportation: the carriages that brought Manchester's employers from suburban homes to city-centre factories (Engels [1845] 1969: 78–79); the streetcars that transformed Boston (Warner 1962); the automobile which has enabled sprawl. As workers moved away, larger concentrations of manufacturing, offices, and commercial spaces developed. Industrial districts, office parks, central business districts, and then suburban shopping malls became possible (P. Scott 2000). The modern city shows varied patterns, including inner-city poverty (Detroit) and affluence (Paris); many people have always worked at, or from, home and more may after COVID-19; some districts contain an intermingling of homes and commercial spaces; in the global South, many still include small-scale industry, notably Mumbai's Dharavi district (Brugmann 2009: 93–103). But, increasingly, metro areas comprise four elements: residential areas, work zones, public spaces, and the connecting infrastructure. That is one consequence of the thoroughgoing separation of work and home.

In economic terms, this separation created modern housing markets. These are local, being defined by commuting fields. To become markets they require many buyers and sellers, a condition only urban areas can satisfy. Then, as happened first in European and then North American cities in the nineteenth century, specialized businesses developed: the land subdivider and developer, the sales agent; the builder, along with specialized trades acting as subcontractors; the building supplier; the appraiser; the mortgage lender. It is no coincidence that leading urban historians have been drawn to the speculative builder/developer, a person who only exists in cities (e.g. Dyos 1961; Davison 1978). As cities grew, specialization increased. It even happened at the lower end in the 1800s, but then building regulations, and rising land values, made this unprofitable. By the 1920s in North America, a new breed of developers created planned suburbs such as Los Angeles' Palos Verdes Estates (Weiss 1987; Fogelson 2005). In the global North, through the twentieth century, lower-income households came to rely on a filtering process, whereby homes built for affluent households became affordable as they deteriorated and were subdivided. Governments came to rely on the filtering process to solve the housing problem (Harris 2013). Agents in the housing market multiplied in number and power, forming associations. The need for developer and buyer finance grew, shaping fiscal policies and eventually financial crises. It is an intriguing counterfactual to imagine what would have happened if, instead of congregating in cities, growing populations had spread evenly across the landscape. They would have needed builders, lenders, and so forth, but nothing quite like the modern housing market could have grown up. The city is, in a sense, the industrial district of housebuilding (Buzzelli and Harris 2006). Arguably, urbanization created the housing market; unquestionably, it has profoundly shaped it.

Innovation

Cities make firms more dynamic as well as more efficient. A durable stereotype is that cities encourage invention and innovation of all sorts (Bairoch 1988: 323–325; Hall 1998; Hietala and Clark 2013). Peter Clark (2009: 13) observes, "from the high Middle Ages cities ... became crucibles for new ideas in banking, manufacturing, patterns of consumption, voluntary and leisure activity, radicalism, architecture, and the use of space and time." Although such creativity has been apparent in many spheres, arguably its greatest impact has been economic. Here, with qualifications (Shearmur et al. 2016), the urban effect has been repeatedly confirmed (Acs 2002; Simmie 2004; Andersson et al.

2011). The point can be illustrated by the industry that is most distinctively urban: land development and housebuilding.

Cities are innovative for several reasons. They encourage competition, keeping people and businesses on their toes (Scott 2000; Rosenthal and Strange 2004: 2143). Lampard (1983: 29) incorporates this insight in his wide-ranging account of how urbanization has mattered over the past two centuries. And then city people have been better educated and, as discussed in the next section, are more open to new ways (Bairoch 1988: 336). Dynamism also arises from the abovementioned 'buzz', which spreads and stimulates new ideas (Storper and Venables 2004). Richard Florida (2005: 1) has argued that it is the concentration of a 'creative class' that has lately allowed creativity to become "the principal driving force in the growth and development of cities, regions and nations." His argument has been challenged for being too exclusive. Paul Chatterton (2000) points out that, apart from the buzz that produces patents and profits, cities 'hum' with everyday creativity. Indeed, it is essential to the survival of, and may be commonest among, the poor

This argument has special relevance in the global South. There, informal activity is often a sign of resourcefulness, sometimes born of desperation (Bryceson 2014; Davies 2019). In such contexts, industrial innovations often occur incrementally on the shop floor rather than in formal laboratories (McCormick and Oyelaran-Oyeyinka 2007). They may even be fostered by the often chaotic patterns of urban development, with different types of land users jumbled together and juxtaposing small, home-based firms (Benjamin 2004). Informal, grassroots initiative is how shantytowns are built, and often serviced, as people scrounge materials, improvise, cooperate, and lobby.

Indeed, housebuilding is a prime example of urban innovation. Notably in the United States, land developers learned that it was profitable to use covenants to set minimum building standards and control who might buy (Weiss 1987; Fogelson 2005). Since the 1970s, they have created innumerable gated communities with shared, semi-private facilities, an idea that has spread across the global South (Herzog 2015). They have learned that manufacturers, offices, and stores were also potential markets (Gillette 1985; Lewis 2008; Forsyth and Crewe 2010). Although criticized for lack of innovation, over centuries builders have developed new methods, including balloon (wood) and then steel framing in Chicago in the 1800s (Harris and Buzzelli 2005). They developed new designs for single-and multi-family living: the English suburban semi, the California bungalow, the Chicago raised cottage, the ranch, and lately the snout house; the Montreal duplex and the Boston triplex, the tenement, the apartment building, and the hotel, whether mundane or grand (e.g. Sutcliffe 1974; Hancock 1980; Oliver et al. 1981; Groth 1994; Biggott 2001; Sandoval-

Strausz 2007; Lane 2015). During booms, some, like America's Levitt brothers, experimented with vertical integration: subdividing and servicing land, selling lumber, as well as on-site construction; but most found subcontracting to be more efficient and less risky. Subcontractors specialized: painters split from paperhangers, who subdivided by fabrics, vinyl, and metallics. All responded to new materials and tools. In North America, since 1900, these included tin roof sheeting, tar paper, concrete block machines, drywall, linoleum, asphalt shingles, Rawlplugs, plywood, latex emulsion, pre-pasted wallpaper, power tools (drills, nail guns, sanders, saws), and, for the home handyman, the Shopsmith (Harris 2012). Retailers reinvented themselves, building showrooms for amateurs, including discriminating women, offering finance and instructional courses. Developers, such as Paul Fauquiau in fin-de-siècle Paris, invented new styles and methods of marketing and indeed whole "reconfigurations in relations between finance, commerce and real estate" (Yates 2015: 2, 5). Lenders have devised new tools, notably the amortizing mortgage. In the global South, developers have found ingenious ways of satisfying the needs of people with low and irregular incomes, creating pirate subdivisions with few or no services, or shell houses that buyers can finish themselves. Many innovations started local and spread; many were reinvented. Change has been relentless, driven by the competitive pressures and the opportunities that cities provide, par excellence.

Arguably, diversified centres are more creative, while the largest places tend to be the first to adopt new ways of doing things. Jane Jacobs (1969) was the first to make the case for diversity, and economists talk about 'Jacobs externalities' (Glaeser et al. 1992; Duranton and Puga 2000, 2001; Desrochers 2001; Krätke 2011: 177–183). She pointed to the serendipity, the cross-industry spillovers, that happens between people and entrepreneurs with different but complementary skills (Bogart 1998). That is why she praised Birmingham. Larger centres are likely to be more diversified, hence creative (Bettencourt et al. 2007; Hall 2000); they have other advantages that encourage the adoption of new techniques. Firms there have easier access to capital, marketing skills, and a large market (Shearmur 2015; Wolfe and Gertler 2016). They become origins and hubs for innovation diffusion in business and local government, as discussed in Section 5 (Pred 1973; Robson 1973: 184).

Of course, some cities are not, or have ceased to be, creative. Perhaps they specialized in declining industries or lost residents to larger centres. More striking are those in regions or nations that are experiencing social strife or environmental damage. The innovativeness of cities is not an iron law – how many of those are there, anyway, in our social world? – just a strong tendency.

Much of the recent evidence on urban innovation challenges assumptions about the effects of telecommunications. Some have suggested that even the tendency may no longer hold. More than half a century ago Webber (1964: 147) insisted that "it is interaction, not place, that is the essence of the city and of city life," which suggested that the telephone and now the Internet and social media have undermined the importance of urban concentration, for businesses as well as people. Currently, the response to COVID-19 indicates that many enterprises can function as employees interact remotely. It is unclear whether this is sustainable, however, and whether it can generate as much creativity as in-person conversation. Neither the telephone nor, until 2020, the Internet had easily undermined urban concentration (Graham 1997; Scott 2006). Many industries value their urban – and often central – location, including corporations needing access to specialized accounting, advertising, legal and consulting services, public relations, designers, and printers. Saskia Sassen (2005) comments that "being in a city becomes synonymous with being in an extremely dense and intense information loop." Florida (2005: 28, emphasis in original) is blunt: "perhaps the greatest of all modern myths is that *geography is dead.*" Riffing on Friedman's (2007) claim that "the world is flat," Rodríguez-Pose and Crescenzi (2008) insist that there are mountains where wealth, innovation, and economic activity concentrate. Cities are still vital places for economic innovation.

Who Benefits?

If companies benefit, workers do too, usually. As Lampard (1983: 11) notes, Adna Weber ([1899] 1963), in his classic survey of nineteenth-century urbanization, discussed the "mutually reinforcing 'cause' and 'effect' of increasing returns to capital and labour": greater efficiency means higher productivity. Whether that translates into higher wages depends on bargaining power. But cities have offered better economic opportunities than rural areas, fuelling rural-urban migration, initially in Europe and white settler colonies, then in Latin America, and lately in sub-Saharan Africa and across Asia (Weber 1963 [1899]: 230–284; Lucassen 2013). Part of the gain for workers is consumed by higher living costs, especially in larger, rapidly growing cities (Hardt and Negri 2009: 153). Underneath all is the rising cost of land. Then, as towns become cities and then metropolitan areas, commuting costs become a burden. This, and the growing cost and importance of education, is why urban birth rates are lower, eroding extended family networks (Mace 2008). Above all, in large cities tenants organize to constrain the powers of landlords to raise rents willy-nilly (e.g. Fogelson 2013). In such ways, the popular benefits of city living depend on political struggles (Section 5).

For potential residents, the advantages of cities go beyond higher, year-round incomes. As Richard Wade (1959: 307) noted, America's frontier offered "widening opportunities." These include being able to choose your employer, taking into account wages, location, working conditions, and benefits. Cities contain a wider range of jobs, enabling residents to develop and profit from innate skills and interests and "permitting a better match between the supply and demand of qualified personnel" (Bairoch 1988: 342). The result is greater job satisfaction. This is especially relevant for women, whose rural role has often been circumscribed to childrearing and domestic labour and who – after long struggles – won greater opportunities first in cities. For those uncertain about what they want to do, who change their mind, or whose skills have become obsolete, cities offer a Plan B. Lately, some writers have argued that creative workers move to cities for quality of life and that firms follow (Florida 2005; Glaeser 2011). There is some truth to this, but most people are drawn to places with the best economic opportunities (Storper 2013). People follow jobs, and that means cities.

Bigger is not always better (Polèse 2009). Smaller urban centres are more affordable, enabling access to more domestic space, shorter commutes, and a slower pace. If the job you want is in a smaller place, or if you can work from home, you can have your cake and eat it. COVID-19 is offering this option to more workers: in the summer of 2020, journalists told stories of families moving from cities to towns, as my nephew has done. Time will tell whether this becomes a long-term trend.

Employers, too, calculate whether a big-city location makes sense. Higher land costs and congestion hurt them as well, so that there can be, in economists' terms, negative returns to size (Bloom et al. 2008; Polèse 2009: 150; cf. Hoselitz 1955). Directly, companies have to pay more for factory, office, or commercial space. Indirectly, they come under pressure to pay higher wages, particularly if workers take advantage of the urban, and perhaps neighbourhood, setting to organize (Weber [1899] 1963: 412, 418–419). As Granovetter (1978) points out, there are thresholds for collective behaviour, including strikes and riots (cf. Harvey 1976). There are many instances where these have mattered, from late nineteenth-century London to 1940s Mombasa (Stedman Jones 1971; Cooper 1987). The net effect of agglomeration, then, depends on complex social and political dynamics. It is to the first of these that we now turn.

4 Urbanism As Ways of Life

In making the city man has remade himself.

Robert Park ([1929] 1967)

Here, new opportunities for communication intersected, new patterns of human relationships began to form, new institutions sprang up, new values, sensations, conventions and problems were expressed.

H. J. Dyos ([1973] 1982b)

Social effects have dominated discussions of the urban question (Saunders 1981; Stevenson 2003; Parker 2004). This is particularly true in the United States, where the influence of the Chicago school of urban sociology, founded by Robert Park, has been huge. In practice, the debate has focused on what Louis Wirth ([1938] 1969a) called "the urban way of life." Historians have shared this emphasis. Jim Dyos's evocation of the significance of the city is typical (e.g. Wade 1959: 309; Handlin 1963: 10; Warner 1968): fine as far as it goes but it leaves an incomplete picture. The purpose of this section is to disentangle the arguments that have been made about the social effects of cities. The most notable concern is the experience of anonymity and freedom, together with the promotion of diversity, social change, and new forms of community, many being influenced by the city's greater scope for social segregation. These are substantial issues but only part of the ways that cities matter.

Economists agree that urban agglomeration has an impact, but there is no consensus among sociologists about the nature, or even the existence, of an urban way of life. In part, this contrast reflects a difference in how widely researchers have cast their net. As noted, the economic literature has neglected the global South. In contrast, sociologists have pondered the social life of pre-industrial cities (e.g. Morris 1968: 39–61), while anthropologists have addressed this subject in the developing world (Berreman 1978; Robinson 2005). One reason why the urban way of life has been actively debated, then, is because it has been explored in more diverse settings.

Yet that is not the root of the matter. Urban agglomeration usually enables economic growth; the exceptions stand out. But the social effects depend on a more evenly balanced mixture of possibilities, varying with personal circumstances and local conditions. Surveying the anthropological literature, Gerald Berreman (1978: 237) makes various observations about the effects of urban size on social life but saves his most telling generalization for last: "other things are never equal."

One crucial variable is the sociocultural setting. Many have argued that the elements usually cited as being intrinsic to city life – personal anonymity, atomism, and associated freedoms – are, in Castells's (1976: 38) words, simply "the cultural expression of modern capitalist industrialization" (Fischer 1972: 217–219; Gans 1972: 42; Saunders 1985: 72). A more general critique has been offered by Philip Abrams. Considering the role of cities in medieval Europe, he argued that "when attended to, the town disappears to be replaced first by numerous particular towns and then by a complex of market, political, and cultural relations which are as it were enacted in towns but not in any exclusive sense of the town" (Abrams 1978: 12). In this view, cities merely express the social relations of the wider society.

It is easy to find geographical examples that confirm this argument. Lately, Chinese cities have offered a way of life for millions that is very different from the experience of urbanism in North America or Europe. For rural-urban migrants, the *hukuo* registration system has created "cultural and institutional barriers that make it all but impossible to become fully-vested members of the urban community" (Campanella 2008: 185). Increasingly, as cameras with facial recognition software are deployed, all urban residents are subject to surveillance. With social lives, and access to services, tightly constrained, the urban way of life is not one of anonymity and freedom.

Social settings also vary historically. Many writers have suggested that, although there was once a distinctively urban way of life in Western cities, that is no longer true. New information and transportation technologies, coupled with urban decentralization, have arguably eroded, if not eliminated, a meaningful urbanism. Eighteen years after he published his classic essay, Wirth ([1956] 1969b: 165) himself noted that "the city has spilled over into the countryside" and that the distinction between urban and rural ways of life were becoming blurred "particularly in the suburbs." Henri Lefebvre (2003: 1) took this to a logical conclusion: "society has been completely urbanized."

Such critiques, however, often work with a simplified line of argument. The stereotype is that cities produce anonymity and atomism. Discovering that this is not the universal experience then becomes proof that there is no such thing as an urban way of life. This is Oscar Lewis's (1952) strategy, in his study of rural-urban migrants to Mexico City, as it is of several American sociologists. The most that Herbert Gans (1972: 42, 44) is willing to concede is that an 'urban' way of life might be experienced by some lower-income residents of inner-city neighbourhoods. But this misses the point. Anonymity and its correlates are only one possibility; urbanism is a characteristic but complex mix.

Anonymity

In a place of any size, it is impossible to know everyone well or indeed at all. Going about our business in our home town we encounter strangers. All we know about them is what we can see – how they appear, dress, and behave – and the same goes in return. Sociologists call these 'secondary' contacts, contrasting with the primary relationships we have with kin and friends, who know our strengths and weaknesses, quirks, interests, and aversions. In between – and there is a continuum – are 'quasi-primary' connections with neighbours, say, or some co-workers. They see parts of us, but not all.

Secondary relations are distinctive to cities (and the experience of travel). In a small community, everyone knows everyone – and everyone's business – via the gossip mill. As villages become towns, and towns cities, the relative importance of secondary relations grows. This, Louis Wirth's ([1938] 1969a: 152) claim, has been borne out. Surveying British community studies Ronald Frankenberg (1970: 282) concluded that "as we move towards the urban end of the continuum redundancy in social relations decreases, social relationships become less complex." At the extreme, secondary relations dominate – everywhere. In a small Indonesian town (pop. 22,000), Clifford Geertz (1965: 33) found an "atomization of social life." Knowing India best, when Berreman (1978) compared settlements his main finding was that larger places offered more anonymity. The same is true in China. There, Robin Visser (2010) describes an emerging urban individualism and anonymity being expressed in the arts.

Writers have waxed eloquent. Raymond Williams (1975: 186) claims these lines of William Blake were "the first expression of what has since become a dominant experience of the city":

> How often, in the overflowing streets,
> Have I gone forwards with the crowd, and said
> Unto myself, "The face of every one
> That passes by me is a mystery!"

Williams (1975: 197, 259–260) notes that Dickens, Carlyle, and Engels ("the brutal indifference, the unfeeling isolation of each in his private interest") soon said much the same. Morton and Lucia White (1962: 41, 47, 49) cite American writers who echoed the theme.

There are indeed people and settings where anonymity is the norm. The centres of cities, especially large ones, can be overwhelming, particularly to recent arrivals who are alone and without connections: everything is noisy, strange; everyone is hurrying about their inscrutable business; no one cares. Here you find a faster pace, "an intensification of nervous stimulation" (Simmel

[1903] 1969: 48). It is hard to handle. You know that you will be judged by your appearance and behaviour (Raban 1973: 75, 77; Sennett 1974). And so, in public, you dress to fit in, to tune out, avert your eyes, block inputs, adopt a blank face, behave with safe predictability, and offer those you encounter 'civil inattention' (Milgram 1970; Lofland 1989; Little 2014: 164–165). In all of this there is self-consciousness, an awareness of public performance (Sennett 1974). This is one quintessential urban experience.

In apparent contradiction, other writers have described village-type communities in urban settings. Oscar Lewis (1952) found this in Mexico City; Herbert Gans (1962) called his study of Italians in Boston's North End, *The Urban Villagers*; Clifford Geertz (1965: 33) reported that atomization was weak in *kampungs*, Indonesian villages that had been encircled by urban growth. A neglected study in this genre is Mary Hollsteiner's (1972) work on Tondo, a large (pop. *c*.40,000), low-income district in Manila, where social life was far from impersonal. Balking at the term 'urban village', because many residents worked outside the area, she nonetheless reported that most people's lives included a web of personal relations.

Hollsteiner's reference to commuting points to a way of reconciling what seem to be contradictory arguments. Anonymity and primary relationships are ends on a continuum and, for most people, coexist. That is why, as Hohenberg and Lees (1995: 265) note, European cities have been both anonymous and "culturally intense." Wirth (1969a) himself recognized that the typical urbanite's life is a mixture because "the individual acquires membership in widely divergent groups" relating to work, residence, and interests. Those of residence include neighbourhood associations, what Morris Janowitz ([1952] 1967) calls communities of 'limited liability'. Such groups help create a familiarly complex experience. 'Third spaces', such as pubs and coffee houses foster community, and sometimes businesses too (Cowan 2005). Hotels, geared to mobile individuals, offer the temporary community of commercialized hospitality (Sandoval-Strausz 2007). A comparable mix is part of the urban experience in the global South, as exemplified by Chanda, Bill Epstein's research assistant in Ndola, Northern Rhodesia: "in any one day he may move through a whole continuum of role relationships, from superficial and segmentary to complex and multi-stranded" (quoted in Pahl 1968: 33). Clyde Mitchell (1987: 301) sees the same across central Africa in the early postcolonial years. In places of any size, secondary relations are an unavoidable element in the urban way of life but, except for recent migrants, they are rarely dominant. Anyone with a job, a family, or even just neighbours is likely to have varied social connections. As the British sociologist R. N. Morris (1968: 163) said, it doesn't matter that some interactions are anonymous "if it is still possible to know all significant others."

Whether the individual perceives anonymity to be good or bad depends. If that is all they know, and they are seeking community, it feels lonely and alienating. That is probably why people in Europe only started to talk about 'loneliness' in the 1800s, as urbanization gathered pace, and why it has featured as a central attribute of urban life ever since (Alberti 2020). But if anonymity is only part of a person's life, or something chosen, it can be liberating. Cities are great places to disappear (Gilfoyle 2006; Moss 2019). That is why the first sections of President Trump's border wall with Mexico were built between El Paso and Cuidad Juárez: when a migrant crosses the border in a remote area the border patrol has hours or days to find them; in the city, police have only minutes (Economist 2019). Those who observe and reflect upon the urban scene might prefer to fade into the scenery, becoming engaged only when they choose. A fine evocation of this experience is Jonathan Raban's (1973) account of street life after he moved to London in the early 1970s. The city is the métier of the flâneur or, more rarely, the flâneuse (Stevenson 2003: 62–64), who "could lose himself in the crowd" (Dyos [1973] 1982b: 7).

Freedom

And so the experience of anonymity can be liberating. It frees people to remake themselves. Raban's London offers possibilities, being "soft ... it awaits the imprint of an identity" (Raban 1973: 9). It is especially welcome for those hemmed in by prevailing norms. The district of Earls Court, a haven for gays – then known as homosexuals – "is a place where people come in order to be free of the sanctions which operate where they live" (Raban 1973: 9, 200). Sukheta Mehta claims something similar for Mumbai, "a place where your caste doesn't matter, where a woman can dine at a restaurant and where you can marry the person of your choice" (quoted in Brand 2009: 37). Mehta overstates the case, but he has a point. Where everyone knows who you are, the pressure to conform can be enormous. In contrast, the city's impersonality promises a "release from traditional restraints" (Handlin 1963: 19).

To this day, gender and race are the most common grounds for being hemmed in or downright oppressed. Women and racialized minorities have often found cities to be preferable. In the global South, women, especially, find cities liberating. As Kenneth Little (1973: 180) observes of 1960s Africa, "urbanization and the women's efforts to better their position go hand in hand" because cities offer "new and extra opportunities of achieving status." A modest income, too, selling produce, clothes, or crafts on the street or being employed in factory work (Chant and McIlwaine 2016: 193–198). The best-documented experiences, however, are American. Single women moved to the city where they "asserted most adamantly . . . their desire for independence from supervision" (Meyerowitz 1988: 140). They rejected traditional roles. Some became sex workers – damned and used as prostitutes – but many more took waged work that offered financial independence. They enjoyed commercial amusements, including dance halls and movie theatres, as well as shopping in department stores, especially once street lighting improved (Peiss 1986; Hickey 2003; Baldwin 2012). To avoid curfews, they chose commercial boarding houses or furnished rooms (Gamber 2007), or they ran the boarding houses, made money as dressmakers, or started grocery stores (Deutsch 2000). And they did versions of all of this in Canada, Britain, and indeed everywhere (Strange 1995; Dennis 2008: 151–163).

Not all was gain. True, those aspiring to marriage now had more options. Moira Weigel (2016: 7) paints the contrast: "Think what a big deal it is when one new single shows up in a Jane Austen novel. Then think how many men a sales girl who worked at Lord and Taylor's in the 1910s would meet every day. You start to appreciate the sense of romantic possibility that going to work in big cities inspired." Parental supervision waned: "dating moved courtship from the home onto the market" (Weigel 2016: 33). But this placed a premium on appearance in anonymous environments like the dance hall, bar, or club. Then, too, opportunities are often constrained. In some cultures, women are prohibited from public spaces. Commonly, domestic responsibilities and lower incomes reduce their mobility and, especially at night, strangers make cities dangerous. To this day, the "greatest inhibition to women's [urban] mobility is their fear of sexual assault" (Spain 2014). Greater choice and freedom can be mixed blessings.

Racialized minorities welcomed city living too, including the most oppressed. Frederick Douglass, an American ex-slave and social reformer, declared that "slavery dislikes a dense population" (quoted in Ellis and Ginsburg 2017: 4). Richard Wade (1964) showed that, for the masters, cities posed problems of control (cf. Goldfield 1982: 45–53). This was especially true for slaves who housed themselves, as opposed to those in 'plantation compounds' attached to the master's house (Vlach 1997). When work was done, they gathered in homes, churches, and grog shops to share experiences and ideas. Wade (1964: 245–246) quotes a southerner: "'The city is no place for niggers. They get strange notions in their heads, and grow discontented" and so, Wade adds, "the cause of slavery's difficulty in the city was the nature of urban society itself." There were nuances. In small towns like Franklin, Tennessee, a slave like 'Henry' had access to the streets for leisure as well as work but was still supervised. As Lisa Tolbert (2017: 147) comments, "white residents, whether they actually owned slaves or not, were authorized to exert substantial power over slave residents." Even so, slaves preferred small-town life over the plantation because of opportunities for unsupervised association. Urban size mattered.

Some urban freedoms were good by any standard. Artists and thinkers have found cities more stimulating, tolerant, or better endowed with rich patrons (Mumford 1961; Goldthwaite 2009). In that vein, Peter Hall (1998) features Florence, Paris, and London. Complementing that account, Paul Wheatley (2001: xvi) has shown how cities were "the principal bearers of Islamic civilization" and indeed the key transmitters of classical knowledge for the West (Moller 2020). Constance Green (1957: 242–243) argues that America's east coast cities originated "the ideas and aspirations that created an urban America" (Green, 1957: 242–243). The urban base of cultural innovation is still apparent. In Canada, Toronto and Montreal are home to the national hubs of cultural production for anglophones and francophones, respectively. And then there are freedoms that almost everyone deplores. Jostling on busy sidewalks and public transport tempted pickpockets (Gilfoyle 2006). Gangs and juvenile delinquency became a thing (Houston 1982). Concentrations of wealth encouraged burglars who disappear into the night, despite security cameras (Baldwin 2012; Moss 2019). Crime does not always increase with city size, but its forms do (Fischer 1995: 561). Anonymity also enables bad behaviour, notably in traffic, "a place where no one knows your name. Anonymity ... acts as a powerful drug ... it encourages aggression" (Vanderbilt 2008: 26). We have all observed this; dare I say, we have all been guilty at some point?

Commonly, however, judgment about new freedoms has depended on point of view. Religion is central to most cultural traditions and, especially when connected with print culture, cities have often fostered a secular outlook (Bridenbaugh [1938] 1973: 67; Fischer 1972: 212). For some, this was liberating; for others, immoral (Boyer 1978; Valverde 1991). In industrial cities, workers enjoyed new freedoms to associate, forming unions but also engaging in rebellious public behaviour, especially at night, attracting concern (Palmer 2000). In Richmond, Virginia, slaves shared drinks while slave-owners grumbled; in London and New York, women made new lives for themselves while men tut-tutted. In America and beyond, conservatives have been critical or skeptical of cities, while social liberals have welcomed them (Lees 1985: 310; Ogorzalek 2018). Similarly polarized judgments became attached to those urban places that enabled freedoms: the apartment and boarding houses, hotels, cafés, and the very streets, although more so in Anglo-America than in Europe, which was less obsessed with the ideal of the single-family home (Marcus 1999; Sandoval-Strausz 2007; Mandell 2019). And the major public spaces of the city became places where, through demonstrations and parades, every movement, group, or party could make its presence felt (Goheen 1998).

There are also some freedoms that attract no particular judgment but simply happen. The new environment requires a vocabulary of alleys and skyscrapers, streetcars (trams) and timetables, traffic lights and stop signs, parking meters and speed bumps, playgrounds and night life, industrial districts and zoning, neighbourhoods and suburbs. The pace and fluidity of city living has produced "an ease of language": neologisms, adaptations, and hybrids (Smakman and Heinrich 2018: 9). This is most true where migrants bring new languages. But even where there is apparent uniformity new things happen. Kohima is a small city (pop. 100,000) in Nagaland, Assam. Almost everyone speaks Naga but, even so, city living has produced linguistic change. Young migrants use *mui* for the first person singular, displacing *ami* within a generation, except among the old (Satyanath 2018). Above all, in cities, no language stands still.

Diversity and Change

These freedoms have added extra diversity to the city's division of labour. Among the butchers and grocers, clerks and lawyers, are some women, some who speak in tongues, and those who are visibly different. More diversity is brought by migrants, looking for freedoms or a higher standard of living. It is hard to disentangle the effects of the city from what social scientists call 'selection bias' – the tendency of those who seek diversity to head to the city (Fischer 1995: 552). But no wonder many have seen heterogeneity as a defining feature of the city. And then, in dense settings, differences are juxtaposed. Jim Dyos ([1973] 1982b: 6) commented that in Victorian cities there was a new "capacity for sustained awareness of other societies or cultures … It was the city which enabled such things to be seen." 'Enabled' is too weak: awareness was unavoidable.

What people make of this awareness is contingent. Many writers have claimed that city life "tends to produce a 'relativistic perspective'" that involves a "toleration of differences" (Wirth 1969a: 155). That is one reason why urbanites are more secular. The writer William Dean Howells reckoned that in turn-of-the-century Paris there were "facilities for every kind of habit or taste, and … everything accepted and understood" (quoted in White and White 1962: 87). Research by North American sociologists bears out this effect (Wessel 2009). It makes sense. Peaceful coexistence demands surface tolerance, 'civil inattention' (Lofland 1989). And when those who are obviously different – in dress, skin colour, behaviour, faith – conform in important ways, while treating others with respect, acceptance may follow.

Yet Berlin in the 1930s; Belfast during 'the Troubles'; Birmingham, England, after Enoch Powell's 'Rivers of Blood' speech; or Ahmedabad during the

Gujarat riots show that diversity does not always produce sweetness and light. The problem is that, even at the best of times, a world of strangers encourages mistrust and fear (Milgram 1970; Fischer 1982: 260; Zukin 1995: 42). There is, here, a "new and complex social order," where "any assumption of a knowable community ... becomes harder and harder to sustain" (Williams 1975: 191, 202). The new environment creates this feeling. Regardless of place of birth, urbanites are less helpful to strangers than those in smaller communities (Stebley 1987). Caution, and initial mistrust, is the basic survival kit in a big city, especially where strongly felt social differences exist.

In good times, diversity is not only tolerated but embraced by borrowing some elements. The examples are endless. Immigration encouraged North Americans to adopt and adapt pizza, Reuben sandwiches, and chop suey, while the British now celebrate chicken tikka masala; both enjoy reggae; burgers have gone global. In Toronto, Nav Bhatia, a Sikh immigrant and die-hard Raptors fan, enjoys shawarma poutine, a (strange) mashup of Middle Eastern and French-Canadian cuisines (Lila 2019). In African cities, rural-urban migrants have adapted traditional practices, including language and tribal beliefs, while adopting or inventing others (Mitchell 1987: 39; Freund 2017: 90–91). In Jakarta, a prospering middle class is buying Western-style homes with interiors that suit traditional socializing: "hybridity behind the Hollywood façade" (Cowherd and Heikkila 2002: 203); in Southeast Asian cities in the 1920s and 1930s, ethnic groups became cosmopolitan by exchanging social practices (Lewis 2016: 10). There is often a class dimension. In nineteenth-century Calcutta, Bengali migrants and their caste superiors created urban cultures but, because the elite copied the British, these fractured a previously shared culture (Banerjee 2019). Similarly, in the Dutch Indies, a Javanese aristocracy imitated "the externals of Dutch life," becoming "cultural middlemen" (Geertz 1965: 82, 83). Commonly, colonial powers imposed standards and practices, as when the British in Singapore defined public space by regulating multi-use verandahs (Yeoh 1996). But sometimes they borrowed. Impressed by indigenous styles, the Dutch developed an *Indische* architecture that embodied a 'mestizo' culture (Wertheim 1964: 173–174). Such borrowings have been common, notably the bungalow (King 1984). In the late colonial period, Western powers developed affordable, hybrid methods of construction. Generalizing about colonial cities in sub-Saharan Africa, Catherine Coquéry-Vidrovitch (2005: 330) observes that cities "have always been rich centers for the encounter and combination, if not synthesis, of values considered traditional ... and the dominant imported values of the time." Imitation is the sincerest form of flattery, but adaptation comes close.

And so, cities bring cultural change. People are freer to be what they are or want to be. Seeing other peoples and ways of being, beliefs and practices change. People may embrace diversity or react against it. Either way, they cannot stay the same. Robert Redfield and Milton Singer ([1954] 1969) suggest that there are two types of cities: heterogenetic, where diversity creates new modes of thought, and orthogenetic, which carry forward a traditional culture. But 'carrying forward' does not mean 'reproducing'. Both types bring change.

Community

One great change that cities supposedly bring is a loss of community, a recurrent concern for centuries (Bender 1978). It is a plausible consequence of anonymity. In fact, what people usually mourn is the decline of familiar forms of community, whether tribal associations, church congregations, or bowling leagues. But cities foster new forms of association, and the net effect is unpredictable.

Many freedoms require like-minded people. Businesses are only viable if many people buy in. Spectator sports, local newspapers, taxis, cinemas, clubs, department stores, supermarkets, and restaurants all depend on substantial patronage (Lampard 1983: 29; Glaeser 2011: 117–126; Beattie 2009: 69). Paying for a good or service often expresses and fosters a common identity (Cohen 2003). That is – or used to be – part of the purpose of the local newspaper, which also informed rural-urban migrants how to behave in the big city (Guarneri 2017); creating community was also an effect of professional sports teams. In both cases, community is good for business. Richard Holt (1989: 167) argues that in Britain from the late 1800s "football clubs provided a new focus for collective urban leisure in industrial towns or cities that were no longer integrated communities." It gave workers something to talk about in pubs, even with strangers. Baseball served the same function in the United States (Barth 1980), where taverns – the 'poor man's club' – served as informal settings where men found community (Bridenbaugh [1938] 1973: 67; Kingsdale 1973). In such ways, a citywide sense of community can emerge, even in places like Bagamoyo, Tanzania, that contain very diverse peoples (Fabian 2019). Often, then, freedom and community go together.

With non-commercial activities, coordination is voluntary and self-conscious. Claude Fischer (1975, 1995) developed a subcultural theory of urbanism which builds on this insight. Wirth (1969a: 151) claimed that large places contain more "potential differentiation." Fischer argues that subcultures in cities are more varied, intense, and often unconventional (Fischer 1975.) They are also more likely to be formalized (Hillery 1968: 304; Berreman 1978) and to have a wider impact, partly because residents are more receptive to new ideas. As Robert Park ([1929] 1967: 18) suggested, "a smaller community sometimes tolerates eccentricity, but the city often rewards it." Most fundamentally, unconventional subcultures thrive in cities because that is where there are enough people to support them (cf. Granovetter 1978).

There are innumerable examples of this, small and large, good and bad. When Michael Frisch tracked the evolution of Springfield, Massachusetts, from town to city in the 1800s, he saw the emergence of one organized group after another, including unions and a Businessmen's Association (Frisch 1972: 245). More generally, by the turn of the twentieth century, "cities figured centrally ... in the growing environmental consciousness," inspiring a movement to protect the American wilderness (Hays 1993; Johnson 2017: 13). Twenty years later, urban change, and a search for community, drove some white southerners to join the Ku Klux Klan (Jackson 1967: 244–246). Often for better, but sometimes for worse, cities have fostered communities of all sorts.

The principle has been operative everywhere, although in different ways. Recreational associations are among the most common type (Hillery 1968: 45). In francophone African colonies, for example, urbanization stimulated new occupational associations and religious practices as well as recreational groups, all of which "reveal an undeniable longing for integration" (Balandier 1956: 506). In British colonial cities, as chiefship eroded, similar groups formed, along with voluntary associations that provided bereavement benefits and entertainment (Banton 1957: 216; cf. Little 1974: 103). Margaret Peil and Pius Sada (1984: 55–58) have interpreted these as subcultures of urbanism. On the Zambian Copperbelt, however, circular (seasonal) migrations meant that urban residents had less opportunity and incentive to develop urban associations (Potts 2010). The same is even more true in China, where millions of migrants lack urban residency rights (Campanella 2008). If urban anonymity is not inevitable then neither is the creation of urban community.

Common or rare, urban networks are distinctive. The involuntary and basic community is the family, but family matters less for city dwellers (Fischer 1982: 258; Jenkins 2013). Extended families erode while nuclear families become idealized. In Canada, for example, Cynthia Comacchio (1999: 56–57) shows that, after the 1850s, as urban life "provided commercialized – and unsupervised – opportunities for amusement" the influence of kin declined. Family remains important, of course, but in cities is less encompassing.

Instead, cities offer voluntary, meaningful association (cf. Gans 1972: 54–56). Migrants can choose whether to adopt urban ways or maintain affiliations back home. But either choice is deliberate, involving "creative improvisation" (Ferguson 1999: 101). And then there are decisions about how many, and which types, of urban community to join – or create. These choices are not uniquely urban, but because the options there are much greater, they loom large. That is why, in his sweeping account of *The Birth of the Modern World, 1780–1914*, Christopher Bayly (2004: 184) sees the rise of the "associational culture" of cities as important to the global story. You don't have to be an urban historian to acknowledge that cities matter, a fact that environmental historians have also recognized (e.g. Mosley 2010).

And then there are pets. Domesticated animals are vital on farms, and some (dogs, horses) became valued co-workers. Yet once horse-drawn vehicles were displaced by electric trolleys, and then by buses and cars, pets became the exemplars of domestication in cities (Robichaud 2019). There, like people, they are policed, with dogs in public having only "the freedom to be led" (Howell 2015). But pets provide companionship and community of a different sort, especially to people who live alone.

Residential Segregation

Community is also nurtured by the residential segregation that cities make possible, even inevitable. As with industrial networks, proximity matters city-wide and also on the block. Here, again, are problems of selection bias: do neighbourhoods foster association, or is it that people who value community choose to live near each other? Whether we are talking about workers or executives, Italians or Muslims, evangelicals or gays, the answer is surely both. Segregation is often chosen but even when involuntary it has an effect (Fischer 1972: 223). Urban scale always matters. As J. B. Jackson (1952) imagined, the elite of Optimo (pop. 10,783) underlined their status by setting up a district with twelve fine homes. Scaling up, in British provincial cities "there might be groups of streets, or neighbourhoods, associated with one social or ethnic group" but "in London – especially in suburban London – there could be whole boroughs in which one class predominated" (Dennis 2000: 104). If cities foster diversity, they also support greater segregation, most apparent at the block scale (Krupka 2007). Wherever we look in urban places, then, concentration matters.

This is most striking where it is mandatory. 'Ghetto' speaks to this and describes the experience of peoples in many settings, including Jews in Europe, South African blacks under apartheid, and African Americans in the United States; it was a routine goal in colonial cities (Duneier 2016; Nightingale 2012; Robinson 1996). Sex segregation in Islamic cities has been no less obligatory (Abu-Lughod 1993). Occupational or class groups have rarely been ghettoized, but housing markets often leave the poor with so little choice that slum living is in effect imposed (Dyos and Reeder 1973; Ward 1989; Mayne 2017). The effects are unpredictable. As noted, concentrations of the poor and/ or marginalized can foster mutual assistance and a sense of community based on shared experience, but it can also enable crime and social dysfunction. What is most unlikely is that it doesn't matter.

The effects of voluntary segregation are more positive. If people choose to live among people like themselves then they must value what is shared and want to reinforce it. Social, economic, and political elites easily set themselves apart. In the late nineteenth century, they created the suburb of Edgbaston in Birmingham, "the [city] council at home" (Cannadine 1977: 472). Developers like to cater to this class, as in Oak Bay in Victoria, BC, and hundreds of other exclusive districts around the world, many being gated (Herzog 2015; McCann 2017). But the commonest enclave is ethnic, and cities are often more segregated by ethnicity than by class. In Montreal's Little Burgundy, for example, there were taverns on every corner and Afro-Canadians – although only a minority in the area – supported jazz clubs, established a Negro Community Centre, a Colored Women's Club, and a Branch of the Universal Negro Improvement Association (High 2019: 27–28). There are hundreds of studies of such enclaves in Britain and North America (e.g. Bodnar et al. 1982), but they have existed wherever cities attracted immigrants. Su Lin Lewis (2016: 8), for example, speaks of "self-segregating" groups in Bangkok, Penang, and Rangoon, notably the Chinese, where place fostered ethnic identity. Immigrants often prefer living beside those who share a language, religion, cuisine, and ways of being, whether to preserve their culture or as a solid stepping stone to assimilation (Conzen 1979; Saunders 2010). How they have accomplished this has been varied, even for the same group, as Jordan Stanger-Ross (2009) showed for Italians in Philadelphia and Toronto. The consequences have been varied: usually positive but always consequential (e.g. Galster 2019).

The importance of segregation has been acknowledged by reformers, politicians, and local elites. They have feared concentrations of the underclass and worked to map, regulate, and disperse them (e.g. Stedman Jones 1971; Vaughan 2018). They have fretted that ghettos, slums, and enclaves may foster immorality or dissent. Even in small cities such as Victorian Halifax, Nova Scotia (pop. 50,000), a cluster of poor Irish and blacks provoked concern and became a target of relief and reform activity (Fingard 1989). Ethnic enclaves inspire doubt about assimilation. Concerns about what Mitchell (1987: 263–277) has called "incapsulation," its opposite, have been widespread. They inspired the North American settlement house movement and 'suburban solution' of the early 1900s and later programs of slum clearance, public housing, and urban renewal (e.g. Carson 1990; Ward 1990). These efforts reflect the belief that segregation can foster the wrong types of association and community.

Such fears have been amplified by the perception that urbanization was eroding the traditional ties that had held societies together. One solution has been to provide services that build social connections: parks, libraries, and especially public schools (Klinenberg 2018). For generations, civic leaders and planners across Europe and North America promoted neighbourhoods, in the hope that these would foster community (Melvin 1987; Schubert 2000; Couperus and Kaal 2016). They designed suburban 'neighbourhood units' and promoted residents' associations to encourage civic engagement (Rohe 2009). The effects were probably limited but speak to the assumption that where people live matters.

It may be that, as personal mobility has increased, the importance of segregation and of neighbourhoods has declined. This would be consistent with the widespread belief that community is on the decline in cities. This belief is reinforced by those historical studies that report a rich associational life in particular neighbourhoods (e.g. von Hoffman 1994) and with recent studies that track civic trends (e.g. Rae 2003). But there is evidence that the impact of mobility and telecommunications has been overrated (Graham 1997; Mok et al. 2010). And, with the growth of financialized homeownership, residents have learned to care more than ever about the value of their home, together with the nearby people and properties that affect that value. The fact that people as varied as elites, immigrants, and gentrifiers still choose to live among people like themselves, and that civic leaders, police, and social activists still fret about conditions in deprived areas, suggests that segregation may matter as much as ever.

Counteracting the impersonal influences of urban life, segregation enables certain types of community, but they are only part of the picture. In the 1970s, Jonathan Raban (1973: 184) reported that "I live in a community whose members are scattered piecemeal around London … the telephone is our primary connection, backed up by the tube line, the bus route, the private car, and a number of restaurants, pubs, and clubs." Today, he would have replaced the telephone with texting but, except during the most rigorous of pandemic lockdowns, cities still offer unparalleled opportunities for association. They do not foster anonymity *or* community: they do both, simultaneously. The effects are complex, unpredictable, and vital elements in a distinctively urban experience.

5 'Urban' Problems and Governance

> It is necessary at the outset to understand what is meant by an 'urban problem'. The chief difficulty … lies in the failure to distinguish those problems that happen to occur in cities from those that are part and parcel of the urban process.
>
> Norman H. Lithwick (1973)

Economic opportunity brings people and businesses to cities, along with social possibilities, but, once everyone is jammed together, they have to deal with the challenge of urban living. Policymakers and editorials call these 'urban problems', but that is sloppy. Half a century ago, the Canadian economist Norman Lithwick pointed out that only some problems are urban in origin. What he might also have pointed out is that others – including poverty, crime, and disease – are exacerbated by the urban setting. Together, they dominate local politics.

Historians, and urbanists of all stripes, know that cities are cornucopias of problems. That is always true but takes particular forms where capitalist forms of property relations are dominant. In the nineteenth century, that was most apparent in Europe and North America but today, with variants, it is true almost everywhere. This matters because 'social costs', broadly defined, are prominent in cities within individualistic, market societies (Morris 1990). They add to the "pressure of urban life" that Arthur Schlesinger ([1949] 1973: 36) perceived in US cities, the "acute pressures within urban society" that Peter Clark and Paul Slack (1976: 15) report even in modest, seventeenth-century English towns, and that innumerable writers have commented on down to the present (e.g. Melosi 2013). This section surveys the distinctive problems that cities face because of the pressure that concentrations of people and economic activities place on the land market, together with the characteristic ways in which local governments, in particular, have responded.

Urban Problems and Externalities

Our familiarity with urban problems obscures nuances and a vital commonality. The nuance, overlooked by Lithwick, is that a meaningful distinction can be made between three types of problems: those for which cities are irrelevant, those they exacerbate, and those they create. The latter two are our concern here. Clustering of people, and their daily activities, makes some pre-existing challenges greater. Poverty is worse in cities, where housing costs are higher, self-provisioning difficult, and the poor are segregated in areas with few opportunities. Similarly, crime thrives where wealth and criminals cluster. In other ways, agglomeration creates new, truly 'urban' challenges. Traffic congestion and waste disposal – these days often taken for granted in the global North – are the most important. As Lewis Mumford (1961: 332) observed, "practices that are quite innocuous in a small population surrounded by open land become filthy when the same number of people crowd together on a single street." Solving them is impossible: at best, we mitigate. But distinguishing between the 'social' and 'urban' types is important because it suggests where intervention can have the greatest effect, whether the nation (and beyond) or the city and metropolitan region.

The commonality underlying both is their origin in negative externalities (Morris 1990). Section 3 discussed the positive externalities that draw businesses and people to cities – the uncompensated advantages of proximity. The downsides also reflect externalities, this time negative. No one compensates the poor for having to pay more in rent, or the driver for having to battle congestion and road rage. Externalities are a fact of life and, by increasing their incidence, urban living raises the stakes.

Depending on where we live, we have different perceptions as to what the greatest costs of urban living are. In large metropolitan areas, congestion is always an issue. Currently in the global North, poverty, crime, and drug abuse draw attention (Gilfoyle 2006; Moss 2019). In the past, and still across the global South, polluted air and water have been dominant concerns. Even if only implicitly, historians and historical geographers have long understood these issues to be urban in nature. They have offered accounts of the health problems caused by the concentrated production of human, animal, and industrial wastes and the ways municipal governments have responded (Luckin 2000; Mosley 2001; Platt 2005; Johnson 2006; Colten 2010; Gandy 2014).

A recent argument is that the negative environmental effects of cities for their residents are outweighed by wider, global benefits (Owen 2009; Glaeser 2011: 199–222; Meyer 2013). This issue has engaged environmental historians such as Stephen Mosley (2010) in his sweeping account of the *Environment in World History*. On a per capita basis, urban residents pollute less and create a smaller carbon footprint because they travel shorter distances and are more likely to walk, bike, or use transit. New Yorkers are the most environment-friendly Americans (Owen 2009). It can even be argued that cities serve a global purpose because limited green space, and the concentration of pollution, raises environmental awareness among their residents (Hays 1993). Certainly, environmental movements have typically originated in cities (Melosi 2000: 106–107; Rome 2001; Johnson 2017). Recognizing this, Ernest Yanarella (2011: 21) has suggested that "the sustainable city" should be regarded as "the true home of humankind."

Inevitably, many disagree. The environmental case for urban living is complicated by threshold effects – the local impact of concentration – which may outweigh general benefits (Meyer 2013). And this may be especially true in the modern era because urbanization enables the relentless drive for growth that is a mark of capitalism and which is at the root of global environmental problems

(Gleeson 2014). I won't try to settle this debate, which is ferociously complex (e.g. Mosley 2010; Douglas et al. 2011; Beauregard 2018; Crume 2019). For now, the significant point is that both sides agree that density matters and that, being human creations, cities should be seen as part of our environment and not somehow apart from it (Reader 2004).

While urban externalities matter at the city scale, they are equally apparent within neighbourhoods and down to the scale of the individual lot, shaping the dynamics of the land market. This market is integral to the city's economy and could have been discussed in Section 3, along with the housing market. But, because externalities are fundamental to how urban land markets work, and because their governance is crucial to their operation, they are treated here.

The Land Market

Worldwide, anyone who has owned city property, while noticing nearby deterioration, upgrading, or redevelopment, is acutely aware of the urban land market. It is peculiar in many ways. The supply of land is finite – indeed, with rising sea levels, shrinking – and so growing demand raises prices permanently. This is notably true for urban land which, despite rampant sprawl, still accounts for only 3 percent of the earth's land surface. Because many people want it, bidding is intense, with prices rising to the limit of what people can afford, after other necessities (food, clothing, transportation) have been covered. Urban land becomes a major repository of wealth, an object of debt, and a large element in national and global finance. Its high price demands governance. Owners are aware of lot boundaries, a potential subject of dispute; because city people move often and the pressures for urban redevelopment are strong, real estate must be fungible. And so, even where, as in Africa and Southeast Asia, customary rights have been common, there is pressure to simplify land ownership by assigning rights to individuals. In Thailand, for example, as Hans-Dieter Evers and Rüdiger Korff (2000: 229) observe, "the market emerges as the main mechanism for the structuration of Bangkok." This market requires agencies that reliably record lot boundaries and ownership rights, above all in places like Hong Kong where the stakes are highest (Nissim 2008: 137).

Urban land is unique in another way: its value depends on relative location, not its quality. It is immobile; every site is unique. Property is susceptible to speculative booms and busts, which can have national and global as well as local repercussions. Within cities, sites accessible to jobs, amenities, and desirable neighbours are worth more (cf. Nightingale 2012: 6–7). Given the high stakes, property owners organize to defend their interests, lobbying for infrastructure and services, or forming NIMBY resistance. In sum, at all scales externality fields define the value of urban land and challenge urban governance for, as (Hans Jacobs and Kurt Paulsen 2009: 135) observe, "planning is fundamentally about the allocation, distribution and alteration of property rights." Many urban and planning historians have acknowledged the importance of the land market, noting the tension between private ownership and public consequences. Indeed, Richard Foglesong (1986: 21) argues that what he calls the "property contradiction" gave birth to planning in the United States, a suggestion that Anthony Sutcliffe (1981: 5) generalizes to Europe (cf. Schuyler 1986: 3–4).

Some social scientists have systematized such insights. In their trilogy on capitalism and globalization, Michael Hardt and Antonio Negri (2009: 155) observe that "in urban environments the value of real estate is determined primarily by externalities," adding that "market failure is the norm." One of the more useful frameworks, developed initially by Shoukry Roweis and Allen Scott (1978) and later elaborated mainly by Scott (1980), speaks of the 'urban land nexus'. This term captures how the value of any site is determined by a complex web of influences for, as Scott and Michael Storper (2015: 8) put it, "urban land is ... simultaneously private and public." Questions have been raised about how this framework can best be applied in the global South, where forms of property ownership vary, and where multiple forms can coexist (Parnell and Robinson 2016). But, regardless of context, with urban land more than any other major commodity, the market demands governance.

Responses

Urban governance usually means the state. Who else can mitigate social problems, regulate traffic and property, and provide infrastructure? In fact, at different times and places some of these tasks were undertaken by other agents and civil society groups, and certainly those groups have often lobbied hard. Yet it is true that the state, chiefly municipal government, has become steadily more important, above all in the largest urban centres.

Many private initiatives have mitigated the 'social' problems that city living exacerbates. The first public responses to poverty – beyond the family, that is – were charity and philanthropy. Individuals and voluntary organizations – including churches, settlement houses, foundations, and a range of civil society organizations – have provided food, shelter, clothing, education, or public facilities such as libraries and recreation centres (Carson 1990; Dupree 2000; Colls and Rodger 2004). Within the land and housing markets, many disputes are resolved by neighbours, or by tenants negotiating with their landlords. Anticipating such disputes, entrepreneurs often take steps to control them.

Developers have maximized profits by organizing space to minimize conflict between neighbours. Landed estates did this in Britain in the nineteenth century and 'community builders' have done likewise in North America since the early twentieth (Cannadine 1977; Weiss 1987; Yelling 2000; Fogelson 2005). In recent decades, they have set up Common Interest Developments, often gated, delegating enforcement of regulations to homeowner associations, a trend that has gone global (McKenzie 2011; Herzog 2015). Occasionally, even in cities, companies solve recruitment problems by housing their workers; more typically, they raise wages or move to cheaper suburban sites, a decision which governments have been encouraging since the late nineteenth century (Hall 1984).

Of course, rather than do the heavy lifting themselves, many enterprises have lobbied governments to do the work. There are innumerable examples. In the United States, having pioneered new types of subdivisions, those community builders went to Washington and got a new federal agency, the Federal Housing Administration, to regulate and guide residential development (Weiss 1987). Insurance companies lobbied for cities to improve fire protection, in effect blackmailing them by refusing to insure some areas (Teaford 1984: 199–202). And then, in diverse ways, entrepreneurs have worked with municipalities through public-private partnerships to undertake redevelopment or, under contract, to provide services such as transit. In modern Nairobi, for example, water and sewerage are (mostly) provided by a municipal agency but 'public' transit is privately run (Mitullah 2018). Government, then, is only part of urban governance.

Yet it is always the most important, and increasingly so. Britain, the first urban nation, set the pattern in the nineteenth century as the municipal corporation became locally dominant (Fraser 1979; see also Morris 2000). In general, "cities desperately need forceful, capable governments to provide clean water, safe neighborhoods, and fast-moving streets" (Glaeser 2011: 95). ('Need', of course, is not the same as 'get'.) Smaller, pre-industrial cities had fewer services than their industrial successors, and since the early 1800s the 'active' as opposed to 'regulatory' functions of city governments have grown (Sjoberg 1960: 245–250; Monkkonen 1988: 107–108). At first, municipalities were mainly concerned with "making swollen cities 'work', not with pioneering proto-welfare states" (Lampard 1983: 39). Most initiatives have been hard-won. A well-known example concerns the American Progressive movement at the turn of the twentieth century (Flanagan 2019). As Roy Lubove (1962: 1) comments, a century earlier New York had "faced the usual, but not yet insuperable, problems characteristic of an urban community: police and fire protection, street and dock maintenance, health and housing regulation." By the

1890s, however, it "required governmental services and controls that the small town could ignore, or leave to the individual, volunteer and amateur" (p. 3). But it took an aroused middle class to make it happen. Much the same has been true everywhere, in places as exotic to New Yorkers as Bangkok, Penang, and Rangoon (Lewis 2016: 47–94).

So how can municipalities meet the challenges of city living? As already implied, there are two main options. They can regulate, to reduce the production or impact of nuisances, or they can provide public infrastructure. A third possibility is to enhance the urban environment to attract businesses and residents, hoping the benefits will outweigh the persistent downsides, but this can create as many problems as it solves.

Regulation and Taxation

Among the first things that cities did was to regulate and tax so as to mitigate, minimize, and ideally prevent the private actions that impose public costs. A basic step was to make some activities illegal and then enforce the law (Gilfoyle 2006; Dennis 2008: 52–79). The first police force was established in a major city, London; by the time Manchester, England, had grown to 50,000 a new police commission had responsibilities for the "supervision of lighting, night-watching, cleansing of streets, and the regulation of traffic" (Lampard 1955: 109). Across Europe and North America, cities of any size recognized that public safety was a basic need in both private and public spaces (Hohenberg and Lees 1995: 319). To be effective, policing, and indeed any type of regulation, required information about people and property. Some individuals and agencies undertook surveys that included photography, mapping, and enumeration, but the task mostly fell to municipalities, in the form of rate books/ assessments, sanitary surveys, and building permits, or to national governments, through censuses and cartographic surveys (Peterson 1983: 23–27; Dennis 2008: 57–112).

In some form, policing of property began long ago, indicating its importance. For centuries much of it involved attempts to regulate 'nuisances' (Valverde 2011). In time it affected building materials to limit the risk of fire, property maintenance, public behaviour, noise, and occupancy, eventually to improve public health (e.g. Schultz 1989: 59–91; Bankoff, Lübken, and Sand 2012). In the twentieth century, land use regulation took the form of zoning in North America and in one respect is unique: it does not reduce the *production* of negative externalities and may even enable their persistence. Industrial zones, tourist districts, and the like do not reduce pollution, truck traffic, or noise but, because the effects of these decline rapidly with distance, enforced segregation reduces their *impact* (Klein and Kantor 1976: 121–127; Schuyler 1986; Hirt 2014). Zoning, of course, has also been used to segregate people, and here the effects have been much more questionable. As discussed in Section 4, some groups choose to be segregated, but zoning has been used to exclude, commonly hurting those who are targeted (Jackson 1985; Nightingale 2012). There is no need to describe such municipal activities at length. Urban researchers, indeed all city residents, are aware of their importance. We just need to remember that they respond to the distinctive problems that arise from city living.

As cities grow, regulation becomes more complex as well as more important. Flexibility is vital because perception of 'nuisances' is partly subjective, while growth creates pressures for redevelopment and land use change. Regulation requires negotiation and compromise – 'seeing like a city' – not authoritarian rule, as illustrated by the way London handled its informal street markets until 1939 (Valverde 2011; Kelley 2019). Nonetheless, in the global North the municipal presence became pervasive. As Stanley Schultz (1989: xiv) observed for US cities, people became aware of "the city as a total environment," bringing interlinked problems that required coordinated response. And so, in Britain and Europe too, it was in this era that urban planning took shape. Many historians have acknowledged that planning responded to the growth of specifically urban problems (Sutcliffe 1981; Peterson 1983; Foglesong 1986; Schaffer 1988; Hall 2002). Others have left the connection implicit, perhaps because it seems obvious (Sies and Silver 1996; Hein 2018), but no one doubts the connection. Here, more clearly than in any other area, historians have acknowledged the existence of the urban variable at work.

Taxation is an alternative, discouraging (or encouraging) rather than prohibiting. Most municipalities rely on a type of property tax to generate revenue, commonly levying different rates. In that way, a type of land use can be discouraged if viewed as disadvantageous. More usefully, they might devise a single tax on land. As Henry George ([1879] 1987) first argued, such a tax holds down the price of land and therefore housing, helping all urban residents. His ideas are still advocated, for example by the Lincoln Institute for Land Policy. A betterment levy is a version of this (Peterson 2009). When land is converted to a more profitable use, its price rises, most dramatically when agricultural land becomes urban. Similarly, with redevelopment, or when public infrastructure is installed, adjacent sites become more valuable, even though the owners have done nothing to earn the increase. This gain, captured privately, is an unearned increment (Hardt and Negri 2009: 253–258). Betterment levies capture it, transferring private profits into public gain and helping to keep land prices down. At the turn of the twentieth century, several governments toyed with this idea (Yelling 2000). In recent years, Singapore has made effective use of it, while China has deployed it widely (Hsing 2010; Bahl, Linn, and Wetzel 2013: 358–359; Haila 2016). In most places, however, the betterment issue "remain[s] largely unresolved" (Sutcliffe 1981).

One reason for this is that there is a symbiotic relationship between municipalities, property owners, and developers: each wants property values to rise, whether to generate higher taxes, capital gains, or profits. In the United States, Harvey Molotch (1976) argues that this symbiosis has created growth coalitions. Its strength is weaker in Europe (Cox 2017) but in some form is almost ubiquitous. That has become especially true recently, as cities have had to compete for investments by businesses and property capital, at both national and global scales (Harvey 1989). This competition may be stronger and more overt than in the past, but it has a long pedigree.

The value of taxes and regulations is most apparent where they are absent or unenforced. When land and betterment are untaxed, housing becomes unaffordable, contributing to homelessness; and when regulations are not enforced, problems multiply. Urban development in the global South often evades regulation, in effect becoming 'informal' (Portes and Haller 2005; Harris 2018). Simplifying, it takes two forms: squatting, where residents have no right to occupy the land; and pirate settlements, where developers sell houses, or partially completed 'shell' homes, where construction is nominally prohibited. Both types are common. For example, having asserted "the essential urbanity of African cities," Paul Jenkins (2013: 21) emphasizes how much informal development has shaped Maputo, Mozambique, a city he knows well. Typically, municipalities lack the means to enforce regulations and perhaps also the political inclination (Ren 2018). Enforcement is often unpopular and, given that many residents cannot afford market housing, turning a blind eye at least allows people to solve their own housing needs. This is especially true in cities that have inherited inappropriate regulations from colonial masters (Mabogunje, Hardoy, and Misra 1978: 9; Dupont et al. 2016; cf. Yeoh 1996). For that reason, and only partly tongue-in-cheek, writers such as Lisa Peattie (1994) have defended slums.

It is an old argument: smart governance can involve knowing when not to act (Joyce 2003). As Stedman Jones (1971: 189) comments, "if sanitary legislation had been efficiently enforced throughout London in the 1860s and 1870s, the crisis in the 1880s would have been much more severe than it actually was." Although now most apparent in the global South, informality was once common in North, as Victoria Kelley's (2019) account of London's street markets nicely illustrates. Indeed, as every building inspector knows, it persists there, taking the form of illegal basement suites and even squatting in vacated buildings (Aguilera and Smart 2017). Informal development, then, is a ubiquitous feature of cities and arguably a distinctively urban feature at that. After all, cities are the most regulated sorts of places, and so they provide the greatest scope for people to break the law and for governments to exercise discretion (Harris 2018; cf. Davies 2019).[1] The result varies. Like the city's blend of anonymity and community, discussed in the previous section, the extent and form taken by informality depends on circumstances. But, whatever the outcome, the tangled combination of problem/regulation/informality is a peculiarly urban conundrum.

Building Infrastructure

Regulations and taxes can address many urban problems but not all: physical infrastructure, too, is needed. We might expect an engineer like Christopher Kennedy (2011: 30) to claim that "to separate the economy of the city from its infrastructure is like asking how the human body would function in the absence of its skeleton and cardiovascular and nervous systems," but he is right. Roads, pipes, wires, and buses serve what some neo-Marxists have called 'collective consumption' while providing 'shareable inputs' for industry, whose value more conventional economists have quantified (Castells 1977; Kessides 1993; Eberts and McMillan 1999).

There is no need to dwell on this, because generations of urban historians (and others) have discussed and documented the importance of infrastructure (Hall 1998; Platt 2005; Reuss and Cutcliffe 2010). Top priorities were the provision of potable water and disposal of human and animal wastes, followed by improved lighting and paved roads, together with traffic management and public transportation, with the provision of green space and social services lagging (e.g. Cheape 1980; Dupree 2000; Nye 2018). The primacy of sanitation is apparent in the historical development of Western cities whether large (Schultz and McShane 1978; Platt 2005; Colten 2010; Gandy 2014), medium (Fraser 1979), or small (Frisch 1972: 172). More recently it has been the bedrock of settlement upgrading programs in the global South (Harris 2020). Typically, projects have borrowed Western technology but sometimes, as in Tianjin, China, hybrid methods have been developed (Rogaski 2004). Regardless, everyone agrees that sound sanitation is "indispensable for the functioning and growth of cities" (Melosi 2000: 1). This, and the later expansion of public health services, explains why cities are now often the healthiest places to live.

---

[1] This argument is plausible only if informality is defined as it has been here. The term is also used in other ways, for example to refer to any type of amateur or substandard construction, whether or not it contravenes regulations.

Historians have shown that the development of infrastructure depended on a series of innovations. Some were political and administrative in character (Monkkonen 1988). Infrastructure is costly, compelling municipalities to devise new ways of raising money. Building and maintaining it requires bureaucracies with new, professional skills. This created pressures, from outside and within, to reform municipal government so that it can respond to widening demands (Fox 1977; Schultz and McShane 1978; Flanagan 2019). The late nineteenth and early twentieth centuries are often seen as decisive, with Birmingham leading the way in Britain (Hennock 1973). In truth, innovation began earlier and continues to the present.

The construction of roads and bridges, together with water, sewer, and electrical networks, depended on innovations in civil and electrical engineering. Necessity was the mother of invention and was felt first in the largest cities (Robson 1973: 184; Sutcliffe 1981: 4–5; Hall 1998). These were not always the very first to develop or adopt a new method: London led the way in building a comprehensive sewer system but Cleveland erected the first traffic light. Generally, however, the association was clear: size mattered. And, as Jane Jacobs (1969: 104) pointed out, each innovation has made it possible for still larger cities to work.

We could end on this positive note but, as Joel Tarr (1996) and others have shown, innovations often solve one problem only to create another. The physical metabolism of the city is at least as complex as the social (Schott, Luckin, and Massard-Gilbaud 2005). When automobiles replaced horses, they reduced animal wastes but increased air pollution; without treatment plants, sewers simply transfer problems downstream, while tall smokestacks spare the lungs of locals at the expense of people further downwind. Because they improve access to clean water, waterworks increase consumption, put pressure on sewer systems, and may encourage urban growth that exhausts aquifers, causing subsidence and, especially in coastal cities, flooding. Building roads eases traffic for a year or so but compounds congestion down the road. Municipalities never solve the problems that urban living creates; at best, they are one step behind.

6 Beyond City Limits: Connections and Comparisons

[T]hrough the greater part of Europe the commerce and manufacture of cities, instead of being the effect, have been the cause and occasion of the improvements and cultivation of the country.

Adam Smith ([1776] 1970: 515)

Up to now, I have talked about a wide variety of effects but without spelling out where they are felt or, to be more precise, how widely. Some are confined to the city itself. This is true of many of the experiences of anonymity and community discussed in Section 4, and of the public initiatives reviewed in Section 5. But some effects are felt by other cities, while, as Adam Smith argued, economic and/or technological change affects everyone, everywhere. Such wider influences depend on geographical connections, and the significance of a city – and of cities in general – depends on the strength and character of those linkages. The first part of this section suggests what types of connections determine the city's influence.

We need to look beyond city limits for another reason. While acknowledging that each city is unique, the three previous sections have argued that all cities can have similar consequences. This is a large claim, and controversial. How can we know that, beneath the myriad and obvious ways in which cities differ – size, density, cultural mix, politics, industrial base, climate, national context, wealth, physical setting – their shared, generically urban aspects have characteristic effects? The answer can only be by looking and comparing. Everyone, researchers included, compares cities. We do so for a variety of reasons but, as I argue in the second half of this section, if we want to confirm that all urban places matter in similar ways then we have no choice but to compare places that are, on the face of it, very different.

Connections

Urban historians, like most students of cities, have not done a good job of tracking the connections between cities or between cities and the wider world (Saunier 2013). Their preferred mode is the case study (Dantas and Hart 2018). After all, seen from the air, the built environment suggests a boundary, however fuzzy, while local archives cover a similarly limited territory. This emphasis is changing, slowly, as indicated by the emerging interest in transnational urban history and the related formation of a professional organization, the Global Urban History Project (Kenny and Madgin 2015; Nightingale 2018; Sandoval-Strausz and Kwak 2018). But 'transnational' does not do full justice to the issue, because many important connections are regional in scale. A prime example is demonstrated by William Cronon (1991: 267), who shows how, from the mid-nineteenth century, Chicago was "shaping the landscape and economy of the [American] midcontinent." Better to speak more generally of connections that are translocal.

Of course, no city was ever an island. At the very least, residents have always depended on agricultural produce and in the process defined local and regional agricultural economies. Chicago was simply doing this on a grand scale. In recent decades, the scale has increased to become global. Torontonians eat blueberries from Peru, Londoners enjoy flowers flown in from Kenya, Beijing politicians enjoy American pork. Some argue that we now live in an era of 'planetary urbanization', by which they mean that non-urban places are in the process becoming effectively urban in character (Brenner and Schmid 2014). That, I think, is going too far. But it is true that there is hardly any place on the planet that is unaffected by cities, as sources of consumer demand, of products, ideas, and finance.

Here we must be careful. It is not 'Toronto' that eats Peruvian blueberries, 'London' (or even 'the City') that provides finance, or 'Beijing' that makes policy but rather, respectively, the consumers, networked companies, and politicians based in those places. Cities, even city governments, are rarely important agents. Yet, as urban places, they do have agency. They help create the socio-cultural environment in which blueberries become desirable year-round; they nurture business and political networks, including lawyers and lobbyists. People and organizations make the decisions that have far-reaching effects, but they do so in local environments that enable and shape their actions.

Local Connections and Among Cities

The connections that cities require and stimulate exist at all scales, including the local. When a rural migrant arrives in an unfamiliar city, the initial experience of anonymity is entirely local. So, to a considerable extent, are the social connections that she makes after a few months or years, whether at a community centre, church, club, or on a playing field. When a municipality builds a sewer line, designs a new master plan, or extends its transit service it is overwhelmingly local residents who will live with the consequences. These are the sorts of local effects that case studies are well-suited to describe.

Some of these effects, especially those having to do with governance, have extended beyond one city's limits to another's. Cities struggle to stay on top of the challenges of size and density and smart governments are alert to good suggestions. In the nineteenth century, British cities were influenced by Birmingham's 'municipal socialism,' "a new vision of the function and nature of the corporation" (Hennock 1973: 172). Soon, as many European nations began to urbanize, their cities exchanged ideas about which services to provide and how (Hietala 1987). Saunier and Ewen (2008: 10) refer to this as a "transnational municipal moment." Zoning, pioneered at that time by German cities, was adopted in Britain and then both adapted and transformed by US cities and suburbs (Sutcliffe 1981; Hirt 2014). Often it is inappropriate to assign credit to a single city. Once an innovation has proven its merits, it is adapted, improved, and recirculated, a process in which many municipalities participate.

In the late nineteenth and early twentieth centuries, some municipal practices were exported by European powers to colonial cities. Although often carried out selectively, improvements such as piped water and sewers were beneficial (Harris 2020). Others, including strict building regulations and enforced segregation, were not (Nightingale 2012). In some cases, colonial cities devised solutions that other places copied. Mombasa's handling of labour strife in the 1940s was one example (Cooper 1987). In the postwar, postcolonial era, new agencies arose to transmit or finance municipal improvements, including the World Bank and UN Habitat. But, regardless, the pattern of influence has tended to be hierarchical, moving from larger to smaller centres. This may reflect power imbalances, but in general it is the larger centres where the pressures of urban governance are greatest and where innovations are first needed.

Connections Beyond City Limits

And then there are urban influences that have diffused well beyond the limits of all cities. Specific cities have effects, as William Cronon (1991) showed for Chicago. Even smaller centres, such as Sapporo, Kanazawa, Niigata, and Okayama, have brought urban influences to their hinterlands (Young 2013: 83–138). More strikingly, Richard Goldthwaite (2009) has shown us the extraordinary influence of Renaissance Florence, where merchants pioneered the innovations in business organization, double-entry bookkeeping, and maritime insurance which became ubiquitous because they generated great wealth, which incidentally enabled patrons to support great artists. Similarly, Tony Wrigley (1967) has argued that, two centuries later, London transformed English society and economy, 1650–1750, laying the groundwork for the Industrial Revolution. It is tempting to focus on such great cities, as Peter Hall (1998) has done. But small places can have perceptible, unique, widespread effects. A recent Netflix (2020) documentary showed how Corsicana, a Texas town of 24,000, became known nationally for its fruitcake and a cheerleading squad.

Yet cities, or more properly urbanization, have collective effects too. For centuries, they shaped rural areas not only by buying produce but by attracting migrants. Their appeal has been underlined by communications media that have become instantaneous and which include movies, TV, and the Internet. Ideas, information, and images promise a better life, encouraging further migrations to, and between, cities (Smith and Eade 2008). Those same media transmit music, together with cultural ideas and practices, that challenge rural ways of life. Some of that same technology extends and improves markets: cell phones enable farmers to keep track daily of market prices; online advertising builds markets for consumer goods produced in urban centres. In many regions, equipment such as tractors, along with pickup trucks, ATVs, and cars, have transformed agricultural productivity and lifeways. And fuelling both production and consumption are financial institutions, invariably based in urban centres, which have helped to make land itself into fungible real estate.

All of these influences are magnified when circulated through networks: that way enterprises and people in cities learn more rapidly from each other (Lees 2000). The connecting web may be regional, as with the Black Country that grew up around Birmingham in the nineteenth century, or the American manufacturing belt that had emerged by the early twentieth century (Allen 1929; Winder 1999). It may be national, as the telegraph and the railroad enabled the American city network to coalesce in the nineteenth century (Pred 1980). It was such networks that cemented the link between industrialization and urbanization that Maury Klein and Harvey Kantor (1976) have shown for the United States and that David Reeder and Richard Rodger (2000) have traced for Britain.

But, for millennia, urban networks have embraced wider horizons. For centuries, and even today, port cities have been vital hubs of trading networks (Hein 2013). They once defined a Mediterranean world (Braudel 1981); before the rise of nation states, in northern Europe, ports organized to form the Hanseatic League (1352–1862) (Sellers 2003). They were vital to the development of white settler colonies such as the United States (Hart 2019). They were no less important for the settlement and exploitation of other colonies, transmitting silver to Spain, spices to the Dutch, sugar and cotton to England, and wealth to all three. The development of steam power extended the reach and tightened the grip (Darwin 2020). At the same time, as Kris Alexanderson (2019) has shown, they also became channels of anticolonial dissent. Then, in the phase of globalization that gathered pace in the postcolonial era, networks of digital finance, trading ports, air freight, and passenger flights have speeded and magnified the economic and cultural influence of cities (Rossi 2017). The temptation is to focus on a handful of 'global' cities (Sassen 2001) or on a larger but finite number of 'world cities' (Friedmann and Wolff 1982), of which Taylor and Derudder (2016) identify 526. But the truth is that no city, and very few places of any sort, is disconnected.

Urban networks have always been structured by power relations. In the colonial era, this was blatant so that, for example, it becomes meaningful to distinguish planning innovations that were borrowed from those that were imposed (Ward 2000; cf. Nightingale 2012). In the postcolonial era, the centres of power are more dispersed and inscrutable although, in whatever cities they may be based, global corporations, the United States, and now China are clearly major sources of influence. Consistently, the West, or today what is called the global North, has been dominant and, in so far as it is possible to judge, has routinely benefited.

Yet if the spoils have not been divided equally, it is clear, as Adam Smith claimed, that urbanization has had wide consequences. Indeed, from Adna Weber ([1899] 1963) through Eric Lampard (1955) to Paul Bairoch (1988), Western observers have seen cities as key agents of economic growth. Until this century, they assumed that this went hand in hand with liberal democracy. The rise of China, and the resurgence of authoritarian tendencies in many countries, has raised questions about that. But it seems that, even in autocracies, cities enable greater prosperity and foster new ways of governing and living (Campanella 2008). Various writers have disentangled the interconnections among these elements, Lewis Mumford (1961) perhaps being the best known. Mumford's geographical focus and perspective was partial in both senses, but there can be little question that his argument – that urbanization, with its myriad economic and cultural effects, has transformed our world – remains true. Yet what gives us the right to make such claims about all cities? After all, they differ greatly and in all sorts of ways. The answer must be to look and compare.

Comparison

Comparison is unavoidable. Every time we describe a place as large, interesting, or well-governed we imply that others are less so. Case studies are replete with such statements, but usually the comparison is implied. When made explicit, it serves to underline just how distinctive a particular place is. Tony Wrigley's (1967) account of London's significance, mentioned in the subsection "Connections Beyond City Limits," builds on the contrasts between the metropolis and other urban centres. Comparison, then, can highlight uniqueness, but that is unhelpful if we are looking for commonalities.

A step in that direction is to view a city as one of a type. There are many possibilities, topical, geographical, and historical. Asa Briggs (1968) wrote about Victorian cities, which included Melbourne, Australia. Innumerable writers have analyzed industrial cities, assuming their shared class structure mattered. More commonly, urban historians have taken the national context to be defining (Levine 2014). And so, we have many accounts of American cities, for example Gunther Barth's (1980) interpretation of a uniquely popular culture. A step down in scale acknowledges the distinctiveness of regional centres, such as those of the American South where race relations defined society and politics (Wade 1964). A step up groups nations into subcontinents, as Su Lin Lewis (2016) does by finding common cosmopolitan cultures in three Southeast Asian cities. Another step goes continental, where Fischer, McCann, and Auyero

(2014) interpret the policy of Latin American governments toward informal settlements in terms of a distinctive blend of populism, authoritarianism, and rapid postwar urbanization. And then, of course, the largest subtypes of cities are those of fraught binaries: socialist/capitalist, developed/developing, or global North/South. As noted in Section 1, until recently the conceptual barrier across that divide has been the highest and most durable of all. Within its confines, writers have generalized about each subtype. Supposedly, if Southern cities are defined by the prevalence of the informal economy, then that implies weak governance. And so Xuefei Ren (2018) looks for commonalities across cities in China, India, and Brazil while Veronique Dupont and associates (2016) add South Africa and Peru to the Brazil–India mix.

In varying degrees, all of these subtypes make sense. Within each, it is meaningful to try to isolate the impact of very particular differences. Industrial cities have attracted a lot of attention along these lines. As noted, Briggs (1968) contrasts the innovativeness of diversified Birmingham with inflexible, specialized Manchester, dominated by large factories; this comparison inspired Jane Jacobs (1969), among others. Joy Parr (1990) explores the twentieth-century significance of gender by comparing two Ontario industrial towns with contrasting labour forces, while Tracy Neumann (2016) compares the political strategies of Hamilton and Pittsburgh, declining steel towns, separated by a national border. Any of the subtypes lend themselves to this sort of treatment. And so, Anthony and Elizabeth Leeds (1976) also examine the significance of national political systems by contrasting the political behaviour of squatters in three Latin American countries. Although it is impossible to control all factors but one, such natural experiments are a good way of exploring the significance of particular elements of the urban scene.

To test general claims about all cities, however, we must look beyond subtypes to compare places that are as different as we can imagine, whether in terms of wealth, culture, politics, or climate. The usefulness of 'most different' comparisons has long been appreciated by some historians, notably Charles Tilly (1984), by urbanists such as Chris Pickvance (1986), and most recently by the economist Richard Davies (2019). However, it is only now that their potential is being more fully explored (Detienne and Lloyd 2006; Ward 2008; Robinson 2011). There are different ways of tackling this. More than a century ago, Adna Weber ([1899] 1963) pioneered the quantitative study of urbanization itself, while also articulating its significance. Subsequently, global surveys of scores of cities have shown that birth rates are lower there (Mace 2008); that, reversing a historical pattern, cities are now relatively healthy places to live (Szreter and Hardy 2000); and, debatably, that they have environmental benefits (Meyer 2013). Such studies confirm the existence of some commonalities but omit many vital aspects of the urban process. For this, qualitative research and interpretations are necessary but, as Kristin Stapleton (2016: 232) observes in her comparative assessment of Chinese cities, more challenging.

An initial, manageable approach is to collect findings on places that are not usually compared. I have done this myself, in global surveys of informal urban development and the history of neighbourhood upgrading. In the first, I argued that, although informality supposedly defines the global South, it continues to exist everywhere, varying in degree and kind (Harris 2018); the second argues that, despite different vocabularies and separated conversations, 'neighbourhood improvement' and 'settlement upgrading' have much in common and derive from the same urban needs (Harris 2020). Such surveys can point to commonalities and highlight gaps in our knowledge. More ambitious are works based on, or which incorporate, original research. A classic approach is to study two places differing in wealth and culture, as Joseph Prestel (2017) does in tracing the patterns of thought typical of Cairo and Berlin, 1860–1910. A related method was that adopted by the Manchester school of anthropologists, who compared what they observed in African cities in the 1960s and 1970s with the arguments and findings of American urban sociologists (Mitchell 1987; cf. Robinson 2005: 45–49). Stefan Krätke (2015) does something similar, combining his own research on Berlin and Singapore with published evidence for Beijing and Hanoi, exploring the varied dynamics of urban industrial districts. Perhaps the most ambitious sort of study draws on both original research and published sources, not only to compare but also to link. A recent example is Carl Nightingale's (2012) account of the rise and global diffusion of the policy of imposed segregation. Here, comparison reveals connections as well as commonalities.

This section has done no more than sketch the urban-centred connections that matter and the forms of comparison best suited to testing the generalizations made in previous sections. Both surveys have underlined the importance of looking beyond city limits and beyond the West. By implication, then, they point to fruitful directions that future research might take.

7 Conclusion

God made the country and man made the town.

Thomas Cowper

God made the cavern and man made the house.

Oliver Wendell Holmes

It is easy to oversimplify; tempting, too. It is a way of making an argument memorable and maybe influential. That is what Cowper and Holmes each did, the one to damn and the other to praise. Many authors have treated cities that way, describing them as sinks of immorality; as hubs of innovation; as soulless, anonymous deserts; as cradles of civilization; as cauldrons of social problems; as our natural home. The truth is that they are all of these and more. Less, too, because everyday reality is both more nuanced and less dramatic than any of these metaphors suggest.

Some things about cities are unavoidable. Walking down the street you will meet more strangers; travelling around, you will have to deal with more crowds and congestion; when you contract a virus, you are likely to infect more people. But many effects are contingent – on the character and situation of individuals or on the organization of society. A place that contains a vibrant mix of social possibilities to one person is a cold, unwelcoming presence to another. In one city, artists and entrepreneurs may cooperate to create a fascinating cultural scene; in another, they may sit in basements and offices and never communicate. The urban environment creates distinctive sorts of opportunities but that is no guarantee that many people, or indeed anyone, will seize them.

That is one reason why it is so difficult to decide what should be counted as a distinctively urban feature. A lack of innovation, or of a widespread feeling of alienation, in one city – or indeed in several – does not prove that these features are not urban. Arguably, these absences simply mean that, in particular contexts, certain urban influences have been counteracted by others. This does not absolve us of the responsibility to track down and document those other influences. To the contrary, it should encourage us to look for them, ideally by making comparisons with places where those features are present or prominent. To that end, as I have suggested, the best strategy is to compare places as different as can be.

Unfortunately, this survey has done this less often than I should have liked. My own knowledge and language skills have limited it to English-language material, and even then there are doubtless omissions. Just as importantly, these works themselves provide uneven coverage of regions, types of places, and topics. We know a lot about major urban centres in Europe and in white settler colonies; much less about the rest of the world and towns everywhere. Right there is an implied agenda for future research. And while I'm about it, I would especially like to put in a plug for historical research on the economic dynamics of those places, paying attention to the character and significance of informal activity, as well as to the flows of information and cultural ideas that have connected all urban places.

Urbanists in general should hope that historians take up such tasks. Writers of fiction such as Alice Munro have repeatedly shown that even a village is a socially complex place. How much more that is true of a town or, obviously, a city. Urban researchers have usually chosen to study small parts of the whole, for example focusing on the social life of specific subgroups in particular areas, the impact of a factory or particular industry, or the politics of a redevelopment project. Putting such things together, and then figuring out their interplay and effects, is a huge challenge. Historical scholars are better fitted for this than most, not only because they are more comfortable with complexity but also because they instinctively look for effects that only become apparent over a period of decades.

Some writers believe that, whatever the debates about the urban question may add to our understanding of nineteenth- and even twentieth-century cities, they throw no useful light on the present and immediate future. True, global urbanization and ubiquitous sprawl are transforming all aspects of the urban scene – economic, social, and political. But density 'mountains' still exist and I have argued that they matter. Face-to-face contacts, and what Mark Granovetter (1973) called 'weak ties', are valued for many types of industry and for the venues of our social and cultural life. Meanwhile, municipalities still have to deal with the consequences.

One large issue was alluded to but has been largely bracketed. There is little question that urbanization has contributed mightily to economic growth. For decades, people assumed that this was an unmitigated blessing. Now, however, many question whether growth, and certainly in its carbon-heavy form, is desirable. By implication this raises new questions about the role and sustainability of cities, too (Parnell 2016). Are they really environmentally friendly, as many claim, or through their effects on growth are they doing more harm than good? That is not a question that many urban historians have had to consider, but it may be the biggest that we all need to think about for the future.

References

Abrams, P. (1978). Towns and economic growth: Some theories and problems. In P. Abrams and E. A. Wrigley, eds, *Towns in Societies*. Cambridge: Cambridge University Press, pp. 9–33.

Abu-Lughod, J. (1993). The Islamic city: Historic myth, Islamic essence, and contemporary relevance. In H. Amirahmadi and S. S. El-Shakhs, eds, *Urban Development in the Muslim World*. New Brunswick, NJ: Center for Urban Policy Research, Rutgers University, pp. 11–36.

Acs, Z. L. (2002). *Innovation and the Growth of Cities*. Cheltenham: Edward Elgar.

Aguilera, T. and A. Smart. (2017). Squatting, North, South and turnabout: A dialogue comparing illegal housing research. In F. Anders and A. Sedlmaier, eds, *Public Goods versus Economic Interests: Global Perspectives on the History of Squatting*. London: Routledge, pp. 29–55.

Alberti, F. B. (2020). *A Biography of Loneliness*. New York: Oxford University Press.

Alexanderson, K. (2019). *Subversive Seas: Anticolonial Networks Across the Twentieth Century Dutch Empire*. Cambridge: Cambridge University Press.

Allen, G. C. (1929). *The Industrial Development of Birmingham and the Black Country*. Hemel Hempstead: Allen & Unwin.

Amato, P. R. (1983). The effects of urbanization on interpersonal behavior. *Journal of Cross-Cultural Psychology* 14(3), 353–367.

Andersson, D., A. E. Andersson, and C. Melander, eds. (2011). *Handbook of Creative Cities*. London: Edward Elgar.

Bahl, R. W., J. F. Linn, and D. L. Wetzel, eds. (2013). *Financing Metropolitan Government in Developing Countries*. Cambridge, MA: Lincoln Institute for Land Policy.

Bairoch, P. (1988). *Cities and Economic Development: From the Dawn of History to the Present*. Chicago: University of Chicago Press.

Balandier, G. (1956). Urbanism in West and Central Africa: The scope and aims of research. In International Africa Institute, ed., *Social Implications of Industrialisation and Urbanisation in Africa South of the Sahara*. Paris: UNESCO, pp. 495–509.

Baldwin, P. (2012). *In the Watches of the Night: Life in the Nocturnal City, 1820–1930*. Chicago: University of Chicago Press.

Banerjee, S. (2019). *The Parlour and the Streets: Elite and Popular Culture in Nineteenth-Century Calcutta*. Chicago: University of Chicago Press.

Bankoff, G., U. Lüken, and J. Sand, eds. (2012). *Flammable Cities: Urban Conflagrations and the Making of the Modern World*. Madison: University of Wisconsin Press.

Banton, M. (1957). *West African City: A Study of Tribal Life in Freetown*. London: Oxford University Press.

Barrett, K. R. (1987). *Work and Community in the Jungle: Chicago's Packinghouse Workers, 1894–1922*. Urbana: University of Illinois Press.

Barrow, H. B. (2015). *Henry Ford's Plan for the American Suburb*. DeKalb: Northern Illinois University Press.

Barth, G. (1980). *City People*. Oxford: Oxford University Press.

Bayly, C. (2004). *The Birth of the Modern World, 1780–1914*. Malden, MA: Blackwell.

Beattie, A. (2009). *False Economy: A Surprising Economic History of the World*. New York: Riverhead.

Beauregard, R. A. (2004). History in urban theory. *Journal of Urban History* 30(4), 627–635.

Beauregard, R. A. (2018). *Cities in and Urban Age: A Dissent*. Chicago: University of Chicago Press.

Becattini, G. (1990). The Marshallian industrial district as a socio-economic notion. In F. Pyke, G. Becattini, and W. Sengenberger, eds, *Industrial Districts and Inter-firm Cooperation in Italy*. Geneva: International Institute for Labour Studies, pp. 37–51.

Bender, T. (1978). *Community and Social Change in America*. Camden, NJ: Rutgers University Press.

Benjamin, S. (2004). Urban land transformation for pro-poor economies. *Geoforum* 35(2), 177–187.

Berreman, G. D. (1978). Scale and social relations. *Current Anthropology* 19(2), 225–245.

Berry, B. J. L. and W. L. Garrison. (1958). The functional bases of the Central Place Hierarchy. *Economic Geography* 34(2), 145–154.

Bettencourt, L. M. A., J. Lobo, D. Helbing, C. Kühnert, and G. B. West. (2007). Growth, innovation, scaling and the pace of life in cities. *Proceedings of the National Academy of Sciences* 104(17), 7301–7306.

Bickford-Smith, V. (2016). *The Emergence of the South African Metropolis*. Cambridge: Cambridge University Press.

Biggott, J. C. (2001). *From Cottage to Bungalow: Houses and the Working Class in Metropolitan Chicago, 1869–1929*. Chicago: University of Chicago Press.

Bloom, D. E., D. Canning, and G. Fink. (2008). Urbanization and the wealth of nations. *Science* 319(5864), 772–775.

Bodnar, J., R. Simon, and M. P. Weber. (1982). *Lives of their Own: Blacks, Italians and Poles in Pittsburgh, 1900–1960*. Urbana: University of Illinois Press.

Bogart, W. T. (1998). *The Economics of Cities and Suburbs*. Upper Saddle River, NJ: Prentice Hall.

Bornstein, M. and H. Bornstein. (1976). The pace of life. *Nature* 259(5544), 557–559.

Bowen, W. M., R. A. Dunn, and D. O. Kasdan. (2010). What is "Urban Studies"? Context, internal structure, and content. *Journal of Urban Affairs* 32(2), 199–227.

Boyer, P. (1978). *Urban Masses and Moral Order in America, 1820–1920*. Cambridge, MA: Harvard University Press.

Brand, S. (2009). *Whole Earth Discipline: An Ecopragmatist Manifesto*. New York: Penguin.

Braudel, F. (1981). *Civilization and Capitalism, 15th. – 18th. Century, Vol. 1: The Structures of Everyday Life. The Limits of the Possible*. New York: Harper & Row.

Bray, D. (2005). *Social Space and Governance in Urban China: The Danwei System from Origins to Reform*. Stanford, CA: Stanford University Press.

Brenner, N. and C. Schmidt. (2014). The "urban age" in question. *International Journal of Urban and Regional Research* 38(3), 731–755.

Bridenbaugh, C. ([1938] 1973). One hundred years of urban growth. In A. B. Callow, ed., *American Urban History: An Interpretative Reader with Commentaries*. New York: Oxford University Press, pp. 57–69.

Bridge, G. and S. Watson. (2011). *New Blackwell Companion to the City*. Chichester: Wiley Blackwell.

Briggs, A. (1968). *Victorian Cities*. Harmondsworth: Penguin.

Brugmann, J. (2009). *Welcome to the Urban Revolution: How Cities Are Changing the World*. London: Bloomsbury.

Bryceson, D. F. (2014). Re-evaluating the influence of urban agglomeration in sub-Saharan Africa. In S. Parnell and S. Oldfield, eds, *The Routledge Handbook on Cities of the South*. London: Routledge, pp. 206–218.

Buder, S. (1967). *Pullman: An Experiment in Industrial Order and Community Planning 1880–1930*. New York: Oxford University Press.

Buzzelli, M. and R. Harris. (2006). Cities as the industrial districts of housebuilding. *International Journal of Urban and Regional Research* 30(4), 894–917.

Campanella, T. A. (2008). *The Concrete Dragon: China's Urban Revolution and What It Means for the World*. Princeton, NJ: Princeton University Press.

Cannadine, D. (1977). Victorian cities: How different? *Social History* 2(4), 457–482.

Cannadine, D. (1982). Urban history in the United Kingdom: The Dyos phenomenon and after. In D. Cannadine and D. Reeder, eds, *Exploring the Urban Past: Essays in Urban History by H. J. Dyos*. Cambridge: Cambridge University Press, pp. 203–221.

Carr, E. H. (1964). *What Is History?* London: Penguin.

Carson, M. (1990). *Settlement Folk: Social Thought and the American Settlement Movement, 1885–1930*. Chicago: University of Chicago Press.

Castells, M. (1976). Is there an urban sociology? In C. Pickvance, ed., *Urban Sociology: Critical Essays*. London: Methuen, pp. 33–59.

Castells, M. (1977). *The Urban Question*. London: Arnold.

Cawthorne, P. (1995). Of networks and markets: The rise and rise of a South Indian town. The example of Tiruppur's cotton knitwear industry. *World Development* 23(1), 43–56.

Champion, A. G. (2007). Defining "urban": The disappearing urban-rural divide. In H. S. Geyer, ed., *International Handbook of Urban Policy: Contentious Global Issues*. Cheltenham: Edward Elgar, pp. 22–37.

Chant, S. and C. McIlwaine. (2016). *Cities, Slums and Gender in the Global South: Towards a Feminised Urban Future*. London: Routledge.

Chatterton, P. (2000). Will the real creative city please stand up? *City* 4(3), 390–397.

Cheape, C. W. (1980). *Moving the Masses: Urban Public Transit in New York, Boston and Philadelphia, 1880–1912*. Cambridge, MA: Harvard University Press.

Clark, P. (2009). *European Cities and Towns, 400–2000*. Oxford: Oxford University Press.

Clark, P. (2013). Introduction. In P. Clark, ed., *Cities in World History*. Oxford: Oxford University Press, pp. 1–24.

Clark, P. and P. Slack. (1976). *English Towns in Transition, 1500–1700*. Oxford: Oxford University Press.

Cohen, L. (2003). *A Consumers' Republic: The Politics of Mass Consumption in Postwar America*. New York: Vintage.

Colls, R. and R. Rodger, eds. (2004). *Cities of Ideas: Civil Society and Urban Governance in Britain, 1800–2000*. Aldershot: Ashgate.

Colten, C. (2010). Waste and pollution: Changing views and environmental consequences. In M. Reuss and S. H. Cutliffe, eds, *The Illusory Boundary: Environment and Technology in History*. Charlottesville: University of Virginia Press, pp. 171–208.

Comacchio, C. R. (1999). *The Infinite Bonds of Family: Domesticity in Canada, 1850–1940*. Toronto: University of Toronto Press.

Conzen, K. N. (1979). Immigrants, immigrant neighborhoods and ethnic identity: Historical issues. *Journal of American History* 66(3), 603–615.

Cooper, F. (1987). *On the African Waterfront: Urban Disorder and the Transformation of Work in Colonial Mombasa*. New Haven, CT: Yale University Press.

Coquéry-Vidrovitch, C. (2005). *The History of African Cities South of the Sahara*. Princeton, NJ: Markus Wiener.

Corey, S. H. and L. K. Boehm. (2011). *The American Urban Reader: History and Theory*. New York: Routledge.

Corfield, P. J. (1982). *The Impact of English Towns 1700–1800*. Oxford: Oxford University Press.

Couperus, S. and H. Kaal. (2016). In search of the social: Neighborhood and community in urban planning in Europe and beyond, 1920–1960. *Journal of Urban History* 42(6), 987–991.

Cowan, B. (2005). *The Social Life of Coffee: The Emergence of the British Coffeehouse*. New Haven, CT: Yale University Press.

Cowherd, R. and E. J. Heikkila. (2002). Orange County, Java: Hybridity, social dualism and an imagined West. In E. J. Heikkila and R. Pizarro, eds, *Southern California and the World*. Westport, CT: Praeger, pp. 195–220.

Cox, K. R. (2017). Revisiting "the city as a growth machine." *Cambridge Journal of Regions, Economy and Society* 10(3), 391–405.

Cronon, W. (1991). *Nature's Metropolis: Chicago and the Great West*. New York: Norton.

Crume, R. (2019). *Urban Health Issues: Exploring the Impact of Big City Living*. Santa Barbara, CA: Greenwood.

Dantas, M. and E. Hart. (2018). Historical approaches to researching the global urban. In J. Harrison and M. Hoyler, eds, *Doing Global Urban Research*. Los Angeles: Sage, pp. 211–224.

Darwin, J. (2020). *Unlocking the World: Port Cities and Globalization in the Age of Steam, 1830–1930*. London: Penguin.

Daunton, M. (2000). Introduction. In M. Daunton, ed., *The Cambridge Urban History of Britain, Vol. 3: 1840–1950*. Cambridge: Cambridge University Press, pp. 1–56.

Davies, R. (2019). *Extreme Economies: What Life at the World's Margins Can Teach Us About Our Own Future*. New York: Farrar, Straus and Giroux.

Davis, D. (2005). Cities in a global context: A brief intellectual history. *International Journal of Urban and Regional Research* 29(1), 92–109.

Davison, G. (1978). *The Rise and Fall of Marvellous Melbourne*. Melbourne: Melbourne University Press.

Dennis, R. (1984). *English Industrial Cities of the Nineteenth Century: A Social Geography*. Cambridge: Cambridge University Press.

Dennis, R. (2000). Modern London. In M. Daunton, ed., *The Cambridge Urban History of Britain, Vol. 3: 1840–1950*. Cambridge: Cambridge University Press, pp. 95–131.

Dennis, R. (2008). *Cities in Modernity: Representations and Productions of Metropolitan Space 1840–1930*. Cambridge: Cambridge University Press.

Desrochers, P. (2001). Local diversity, human creativity and technological innovation. *Growth and Change* 32(3), 369–394.

Detienne, M. and J. Lloyd. (2006). Doing comparative anthropology in the field of politics. *Arion: A Journal of Humanities and the Classics. Third Series*, 32 (3), 67–86.

Deutsch, S. (2000). *Women and the City: Gender, Power and Space in Boston, 1870–1940*. New York: Oxford University Press.

Douglas, I., D. Goode, M. Houck, and R. Wang, eds. (2011). *The Routledge Handbook of Urban Ecology*. New York: Routledge.

Du, J. (2020). *The Shenzhen Experiment: The Story of China's Instant City*. Cambridge, MA: Harvard University Press.

Duneier, M. (2016). *Ghetto: The Invention of a Place, the History of an Idea*. New York: Farrar, Straus and Giroux.

Dupont, V., D. Jordhus-Lier, C. Sutherland, and E. Braathen, eds. (2016). *Politics of Slums in the Global South: Urban Informality in Brazil, India, South Africa and Peru*. London: Routledge.

Dupree, M. (2000). The provision of social services. In M. Daunton, ed., *The Cambridge Urban History of Britain, Vol. 3: 1840–1950*. Cambridge: Cambridge University Press, pp. 351–394.

Duranton, G. and D. Puga. (2000). Diversity and specialization in cities: Why, where, and when does it matter? *Urban Studies* 37(3), 533–535.

Duranton, G. and D. Puga. (2001). "Nursery cities": Urban diversity, process innovation, and the life cycles of products. *American Economic Review* 91 (5), 1454–1477.

Dyos, H. J. (1961). *Victorian Suburb: A Study of the Growth of Camberwell*. Leicester: Leicester University Press.

Dyos, H. J. ([1973] 1982a). Urbanity and suburbanity. In D. Cannadine and D. Reeder, eds, *Exploring the Urban Past: Essays in Urban History by H.J. Dyos*. Cambridge: Cambridge University Press, pp. 19–36.

Dyos, H. J. ([1973] 1982b). The Victorian city in historical perspective. In D. Cannadine and D. Reeder, eds, *Exploring the Urban Past: Essays in*

Urban History by H.J. Dyos. Cambridge: Cambridge University Press, pp. 3–18.

Dyos, H. J. ([1969] 1982). Some historical reflections on the quality of urban life. In D. Cannadine and D. Reeder, eds, *Exploring the Urban Past: Essays in Urban History by H.J. Dyos*. Cambridge: Cambridge University Press, pp. 56–78.

Dyos, H. J. and D. Reeder. (1973). Slums and suburbs. In H. J. Dyos and M. Wolff, eds, *The Victorian City: Images and Realities, Vol. 2: Shapes on the Ground and a Change of Accent*. London: Routledge and Kegan Paul, pp. 359–386.

Eberts, R. W. and D. P. McMillan. (1999). Agglomeration economies and urban public infrastructure. In E. S. Mills and P. Cheshire, eds, *Handbook of Regional and Urban Economics*, Vol. 3. Amsterdam: Elsevier, pp. 1455–1495.

Economist (2019). Borderline disorder. *The Economist*, 21 December.

Ellis, C. and R. Ginsburg, eds. (2017). *Slavery in the City: Architecture and Landscapes of Urban Slavery in North America*. Charlottesville: University of Virginia Press.

Engels, F. ([1845] 1969). *The Condition of the Working Class in England*. St Albans: Panther.

Evers, H.-D. and R. Korff. (2000). *Southeast Asian Urbanism: The Meaning and Power of Social Space*. New York: St. Martin's Press.

Ewen, S. (2016). *What Is Urban History?* Cambridge: Polity Press.

Fabian, S. (2019). *Making Identity on the Swahili Coast: Urban Life, Community and Belonging in Bagamoyo*. Cambridge: Cambridge University Press.

Ferguson, J. (1999). *Expectations of Modernity: Myths and Meanings of Urban life on the Zambian Copperbelt*. Berkeley: University of California Press.

Fingard, J. (1989). *The Dark Side of Life in Victorian Halifax*. Porters Lake, NS: Pottersfield Press.

Fischer, B., B. McCann, and J. Auyero, eds. (2014). *Cities from Scratch: Poverty and Informality in Urban Latin America*. Durham, NC: Duke University Press.

Fischer, C. (1972). Urbanism as a way of life: A review and agenda. *Sociological Methods and Research* 1(2), 181–242.

Fischer, C. (1975). Toward a subcultural theory of urbanism. *American Journal of Sociology* 80(6), 1319–1341.

Fischer, C. (1982). *To Dwell Among Friends: Personal Networks in Town and City*. Chicago: University of Chicago Press.

Fischer, C. (1995). The subcultural theory of urbanism: A twentieth-year assessment. *American Journal of Sociology* 101(3), 543–577.

Flanagan, M. (2019). Progressives and Progressivism in an era of reform. In T. Gilfoyle, ed., *The Oxford Encyclopedia of American Urban History*. New York: Oxford University Press, pp. 179–197.

Florida, R. (2005). *Cities and the Creative Class*. London: Routledge.

Fogelson, R. M. (2005). *Bourgeois Nightmares: Suburbia, 1870–1930*. New Haven, CT: Yale University Press.

Fogelson, R. M. (2013). *The Great Rent Wars: New York, 1917–1929*. New Haven, CT: Yale University Press.

Foglesong, R. F. (1986). *Planning the Capitalist City: The Colonial Era to the 1920s*. Princeton, NJ: Princeton University Press.

Forsyth, A. and K. Crewe. (2010). Suburban technopoles as places: The international-campus-garden-suburb style. *Urban Design International* 15 (3), 165–182.

Fox, K. (1977). *Better City Government: Innovation in American Urban Politics, 1850–1937*. Philadelphia: Temple University Press.

Frankenberg, R. (1970). *Communities in Britain: Social Life in Town and Country*, rev. ed. Harmondsworth, UK: Penguin.

Fraser, D. (1979). *Power and Authority in the Victorian City*. Oxford: Basil Blackwell.

Fraser, D. and A. Sutcliffe. (1983). Introduction. In D. Fraser and A. Sutcliffe, eds, *The Pursuit of Urban History*. London: Arnold, pp. xi–xxx.

Freund, B. (2017). *The African City: A History*. Cambridge: Cambridge University Press.

Friedman, T. L. (2007). *The World Is Flat: A Brief History of the Twenty-First Century*. New York: Farrar, Straus and Giroux.

Friedmann, J. (2002). *The Prospect of Cities*. Minneapolis: University of Minnesota Press.

Friedmann, J. and G. Wolff. (1982). World city formation: An agenda for research and action. *International Journal of Urban and Regional Research* 6(3), 309–344.

Frisch, M. H. (1972). *Town into City: Springfield, Massachusetts, and the Meaning of Community, 1840–1880*. Cambridge, MA: Harvard University Press.

Frost, L. (1998). The contribution of the urban sector to Australian economic development before 1914. *Australian Economic History Review* 38(1), 42–73.

Galster, G. C. (2019). *Making Our Neighborhoods, Making Our Selves*. Chicago: University of Chicago Press.

Gamber, W. (2007). *The Boardinghouse in Nineteenth-Century America*. Baltimore: Johns Hopkins University Press.

Gandy, M. (2014). *The Fabric of Space: Water, Modernity, and the Urban Imagination*. Cambridge, MA: MIT Press.

Gans, H. G. (1962). *The Urban Villagers: Group and Class in the Life of Italian-Americans*. New York: Free Press of Glencoe.

Gans, H. G. ([1962] 1972). Urbanism and suburbanism as ways of life: A re-evaluation of definitions. In H. G. Gans, *People and Plans: Essays on Urban Problems and Solutions*. Harmondsworth: Penguin, pp. 41–6.

Geertz, C. (1965). *The Social History of an Indonesian Town*. Cambridge, MA: MIT Press.

George, H. ([1879] 1987). *Progress and Poverty*. New York: Robert Schalkenbach Foundation.

Gilfoyle, T. (1998). White cities, linguistic turns and Disneylands: The new paradigms of urban history. *Reviews in American History* 26(1), 175–204.

Gilfoyle, T. (2006). *A Pickpocket's Tale: The Underworld of Nineteenth Century New York*. New York: W.W. Norton.

Gilfoyle, T., ed. (2019). *The Oxford Encyclopedia of American Urban History*. New York: Oxford University Press.

Gillette, H. (1985). The evolution of the planned shopping center in suburb and city. *Journal of the American Planning Association* 51(4), 449–460.

Glaeser, E. L. (2011). *Triumph of the City: How Our Greatest Invention Makes Us Richer, Smarter, Greener, and Happier*. New York: Penguin.

Glaeser, E. L., H. D. Kallal, J. A. Scheinkman, and A. Shleifer. (1992). Growth in cities. *Journal of Political Economy* 100(6), 1126–1152.

Gleeson, B. (2014). *The Urban Condition*. New York: Routledge.

Goheen, P. (1974). Interpreting the American city: Some historical perspectives. *Geographical Review* 64(3), 362–384.

Goheen, P. (1986). Urban historical geography: A 1985 report card. *Urban Geography* 7(3), 258–262.

Goheen, P. (1998). Public space and the geography of the modern city. *Progress in Human Geography* 22(4), 479–496.

Goldfield, D. R. (1982). *Cotton Fields and Skyscrapers: Southern City and Region 1607–1980*. Baltimore: Johns Hopkins University Press.

Goldthwaite, R. A. (2009). *The Economy of Renaissance Florence*. Baltimore: Johns Hopkins University Press.

Graham, S. (1997). Cities in the real-time age: The paradigm challenge of telecommunications to the conception of planning of urban space. *Environment and Planning A* 29(1), 105–127.

Granovetter, M. (1973). The strength of weak ties. *American Journal of Sociology* 78(6), 1360–1380.

Granovetter, M. (1978). Threshold models of collective behavior. *American Journal of Sociology* 83(6), 1420–1443.

Granovetter, M. (1985). Economic action and social structures: The problem of embeddedness. *American Journal of Sociology* 91(3), 481–510.

Gras, N. S. B. (1925). The rise of the metropolitan community. In E. W. Burgess, ed., *The Urban Community*. Chicago: University of Chicago Press, pp. 183–191.

Green, C. M. (1957). *American Cities in the Growth of the Nation*. New York: Harper & Row.

Green, H. (2019). Company towns in the United States. In T. Gilfoyle, ed., *The Oxford Encyclopedia of American Urban History*. New York: Oxford University Press, pp. 86–102.

Green, N. (1997). *Ready-to-Wear and Ready-to-Work: A Century of Industry and Immigrants in Paris and New York*. Durham, NC: Duke University Press.

Groth, P. (1994). *Living Downtown: The History of Residential Hotels in the United States*. Berkeley: University of California Press.

Guarneri, J. (2017). *Newsprint Metropolis: City Papers and the Making of Modern Americans*. Chicago: University of Chicago Press.

Gunn, S. (2001). The spatial turn: Changing histories of space and time. In S. Gunn and R. J. Morris, eds, *Identities in Space: Contested Terrains in the Western City since 1850*. Aldershot: Ashgate, pp. 1–14.

Haila, A. (2016). *Urban Land Rent: Singapore As a Property State*. Chichester: Wiley-Blackwell.

Hall, P. (1984). Metropolis 1890–1940: Challenges and responses. In A. Sutcliffe, ed., *Metropolis 1890–1940*. London: Mansell, pp. 19–66.

Hall, P. (1998). *Cities in Civilization: Culture, Innovation and Urban Order*. London: Wiedenfeld and Nelson.

Hall, P. (2000). Creative cities: Cities and economic development. *Urban Studies* 37(4), 639–649.

Hall, P. (2002). *Cities of Tomorrow: An Intellectual History of Urban Planning and Design in the Twentieth Century*. Cambridge, MA: Blackwell.

Hancock, J. (1980). The apartment house in urban America. In A. D. King, ed., *Buildings and Society*. London: Routledge and Kegan Paul.

Handlin, O. (1963). The modern city as a field of historical study. In O. Handlin and J. Burchard, eds, *The Historian and the City*. Cambridge, MA: MIT Press, pp. 1–26.

Hardt, M. and A. Negri. (2009). *Commonwealth*. Cambridge, MA: Belknap Press.

Harris, R. (2012). *Building a Market: The Rise of the Home Improvement industry, 1914–1960*. Chicago: University of Chicago Press

Harris, R. (2013). The rise of filtering down: The American housing market transformed, 1918–1929. *Social Science History* 37(4), 515–549.

Harris, R. (2018). Modes of informal urban development: A global phenomenon. *Journal of Planning Literature* 33(3), 267–286.

Harris, R. (2019). A portrait of North American urban historians. *Journal of Urban History* 45(6), 1237–1245

Harris, R. (2020). Neighbourhood upgrading: A fragmented global history. *Progress in Planning* 142, 1–30.

Harris, R. and M. Buzzelli. (2005). House building in the Machine Age, 1920s–1970s: Realities and perceptions of modernization in North America and Australia. *Business History* 47(1), 59–85.

Harris, R. and R. Lewis. (1998). How the past matters: North American cities in the twentieth century. *Journal of Urban Affairs* 20(2),159–174.

Harris, R. and M. Smith. (2011). The history in urban studies. A comment. *Journal of Urban Affairs* 32(1), 99–105.

Hart, E. (2019). Seaport cities in North America, 1600–1800. In T. Gilfoyle, ed., *The Oxford Encyclopedia of American Urban History*, pp. 21–37.

Harvey, D. (1976). Labor, capital and class struggle around the built environment. *Politics and Society* 6(3), 265–295.

Harvey, D. (1985). Money, time, space and the city. In D. Harvey, *Consciousness and the Urban Experience: Studies in the History and Theory of Capitalist Urbanization*. Baltimore: Johns Hopkins University Press, pp. 1–35.

Harvey, D. (1989). From managerialism to entrepreneurialism: The transformation of urban governance in late capitalism. *Geografiska Annaler* 71B(1), 3–17.

Hays, S. P. (1993). From the history of the city to the history of the urbanized society. *Journal of Urban History* 19(4), 3–25.

Hein, C. (2013). Port cities. In P. Clark, ed., *The Oxford Handbook of Cities in World History*. Oxford: Oxford University Press.

Hein, C. (2018). *The Routledge Handbook of Planning History*. London: Routledge.

Henderson, J. V. (1988). *Urban Development: Theory, Fact and Illusion*. New York: Oxford University Press.

Henley, J. (2019). The Norwegian island that abolished time. *The Guardian*, June 20.

Hennock, E. P. (1973). *Fit and Proper Persons: Ideal and Reality in 19th Century Urban Government*. London: Arnold.

Hershberg, T. (1981). *Philadelphia: Work, Space, Family and Group Experiences in the Nineteenth Century*. New York: Oxford University Press.

Herzog, L. A. (2015). *Global Suburbs: Urban Sprawl from the Rio Grande to Rio de Janeiro*. New York: Routledge.

Hickey, G. (2003). *Hope and Danger in the New South City*. Athens: University of Georgia Press.

Hietala, M. (1987). *Services and Urbanization at the Turn of the Century: The Diffusion of Innovations*. Helsinki: Suomen Historiallinen Sewa.

Hietala, M. and Clark, P. (2013). Creative cities. In P. Clark, ed., *Cities in World History*. Oxford: Oxford University Press, pp. 720–736.

High, S. (2019). Little Burgundy: The interwoven histories of race, residence, and work in twentieth-century Montreal. *Urban History Review* 46(1), 23–44.

Hillery, G. A. (1968). *Communal Organizations: A Study of Local Societies*. Chicago: University of Chicago Press.

Hirt, S. (2014). *Zoned in the USA: The Origins and Implications of American Land Use Regulation*. Ithaca, NY: Cornell University Press.

Hohenberg, P. (2004). The historical geography of European cities: An interpretative essay. In J. V. Henderson and J.-F. Thisse, eds, *Handbook of Regional and Urban Economics, Vol. 4: Cities and Geography*. Amsterdam: Elsevier, pp. 3021–3052.

Hohenberg, P. M. and L. H. Lees. (1995). *The Making of Urban Europe: 1000–1994*. Cambridge, MA: Harvard University Press.

Hollsteiner, M. R. (1972). Becoming an urbanite: The neighbourhood as a learning environment. In D. J. Dwyer, ed., *The City As a Centre of Change in Asia*. Hong Kong: Hong Kong University Press, pp. 29–40.

Holt, R. (1989). *Sport and the British: A Modern History*. New York: Oxford University Press.

Hoover, E. M. (1948). *The Location of Economic Activity*. New York: McGraw-Hill.

Hoselitz, B. F. (1955). Generative and parasitic cities. *Economic Development and Cultural Change* 3(3), 278–294.

Houston, S. E. (1982). The "waifs and strays" of a late Victorian city: Juvenile delinquents in Toronto. In J. Parr, ed., *Childhood and Family in Canadian History*. Toronto: McClelland and Stewart, pp. 129–142.

Howell, P. (2015). *At Home and Astray: The Domestic Dog in Victorian Britain*. Charlottesville: University of Virginia Press.

Hsing, Y.-T. (2010). *The Great Urban Transformation: Politics of Land and Property in China*. New York: Oxford University Press.

Hubbard, P. (2006). *The City*. New York: Routledge.

Hung, H.-F. and Zhan, S. (2013). Industrialization and the city: East and West. In P. Clark, ed., *Cities in World History*. Oxford: Oxford University Press, pp. 645–663.

Jackson, J. B. (1952). The almost perfect town. *Landscape* 2(1), 2–8.

Jackson, K. T. (1967). *The Ku Klux Klan in the City, 1915–1930*. New York: Oxford University Press.

Jackson, K. T. (1985). *Crabgrass Frontier: The Suburbanization of the United States*. New York: Oxford University Press.

Jacobs, H. M. and K. Paulsen. (2009). Property rights: The neglected theme of 20th century American Planning. *Journal of the American Planning Association* 75(2), 134–143.

Jacobs, J. (1969). *The Economy of Cities*. New York: Vintage.

Janowitz, M. ([1952] 1967). *The Community Press in an Urban Setting: The Social Elements of Urbanism*. Chicago: University of Chicago Press.

Jansen, H. S. (1996). Wrestling with the angel: Problems of definition in urban historiography. *Urban History* 23(3), 277–299.

Jenkins, P. (2013). *Urbanization, Urbanism and Urbanity in an African City: Home Spaces and Home Cultures*. Basingstoke: Palgrave Macmillan.

Johnson, N. H. (2017). *Escaping the Dark, Gray City: Fear and Hope in Progressive-Era Conservation*. New Haven, CT: Yale University Press.

Johnson, S. (2006). *The Ghost Map: The Story of London's Most Terrifying Epidemic – and How it Changed Science, Cities, and the Modern World*. New York: Riverhead.

Joyce, P. (2003). *Rule of Freedom: Liberalism and the Modern City*. London: Verso.

Kelley, V. (2019). *Cheap Street: London's Street Markets and the Cultures of Informality, c1850–1939*. Manchester: Manchester University Press.

Kennedy, C. (2011). *The Evolution of Great World Cities: Urban Wealth and Economic Growth*. Toronto: Rotman-UTP Publishing.

Kenny, N. and R. Madgin. (2015). "Every time I describe a city": Urban history as comparative and transnational practice. In N. Kenny and R. Madgin, eds, *Cities Beyond Borders: Comparative and Transnational Approaches to Urban History*. Burlington, VT: Ashgate, pp. 3–26.

Kessides, C. (1993). *The Contributions of Infrastructure to Economic Development: A Review of Experience and Policy Implications*. Washington, DC: World Bank.

Kim, J. (2019). *Imperial Metropolis: Los Angeles, Mexico, and the Borderlands of the American Empire, 1865–1941*. Chapel Hill: University of North Carolina Press.

King, A. D. (1984). *The Bungalow: The Production of a Global Culture.* London: Routledge and Kegan Paul.

Kingsdale, J. M. (1973). The "poor man's club": Social functions of the urban working-class saloon. *American Quarterly* 25(4), 472–489.

Klein, M. and H. A. Kantor. (1976). *Prisoners of Progress: American Industrial Cities 1850–1920.* New York: Macmillan.

Klinenberg, E. (2018). *Palaces for the People: How Social Infrastructure Can Help Fight Inequality, Polarization, and the Decline of Civic Life.* New York: Crown.

Krätke, S. (2011). *The Creative Capital of Cities: Interactive Knowledge Creation and the Urbanization Economies of Innovation.* Chichester: Wiley-Blackwell.

Krätke, S. (2015). New economies, new spaces. In R. Paddison and T. Hutton, eds, *Cities and Economic Change: Restructuring and Dislocation in the Global Metropolis.* Los Angeles: Sage, pp. 57–73.

Krugman, P. (1991). Increasing returns and economic geography. *Journal of Political Economy* 99(3), 483–499.

Krupka, D. J. (2007). Are big cities more segregated? Neighbourhood scale and the measurement of segregation. *Urban Studies* 44(1), 187–197.

Kwak, N. H. (2018). History. In D. Iossifora, C. N. H. Doll, and A. Gasparados, eds., *Defining the Urban: Interdisciplinary and Professional Perspectives.* London: Routledge, pp. 53–62.

Lampard, E. E. (1955). The history of cities in the economically advanced areas. *Economic Development and Cultural Change* 3(2), 81–136.

Lampard, E. E. (1961). American historians and the study of urbanization. *American Historical Review* 67(1), 49–61.

Lampard, E. E. (1983). The nature of urbanization. In D. Fraser and A. Sutcliffe, eds, *The Pursuit of Urban History.* London: Arnold, pp. 3–53.

Landes, D. (1983). *Revolution in Time: Clocks and the Making of the Modern World.* Cambridge, MA: Belknap Press.

Lane, B. (2015). *Houses for a New World: Builders and Buyers in American Suburbs 1945–1965.* Princeton, NJ: Princeton University Press.

Lang, R. E. (2003). *Edgeless Cities: Exploring the Elusive Metropolis.* Washington, DC: Brookings Institution Press.

Leeds, A. and E. Leeds (1976). Accounting for behavioral differences: Three political systems and the responses to squatters in Brazil, Peru, and Chile. In J. Walton and L. H. Masotti, eds, *The City in Comparative Perspective.* Beverley Hills: Sage, pp. 193–248.

Lees, A. (1985). *Cities Perceived: Urban Society in European and American Thought, 1820–1940.* New York: Columbia University Press.

Lees, A. and L. H. Lees. (2007). *Cities and the Making of Modern Europe, 1750–1914*. Cambridge: Cambridge University Press.

Lees, L. H. (2000). Urban networks. In M. Daunton, ed., *The Cambridge Urban History of Britain, Vol. 3: 1840–1950*. Cambridge: Cambridge University Press, pp. 59–94.

Lefebvre, H. (2003). *The Urban Revolution*. Minneapolis, MN: University of Minnesota Press.

Levine, P. (2014). Is comparative history possible? *History and Theory* 53(3), 331–347.

Levine, R. (1997). *A Geography of Time*. New York: Basic Books.

Levinson, M. (2006). *The Box: How the Shipping Container Made the World Smaller and the World Economy Bigger*. Princeton: Princeton University Press.

Lewis, O. (1952). Urbanization without breakdown. *Scientific Monthly* 75, 31–41.

Lewis, R. (2000). *Manufacturing Montreal: The Making of an Industrial Landscape, 1850–1930*. Baltimore: Johns Hopkins University Press.

Lewis, R. (2008). *Chicago Made: Factory Networks in the Industrial Metropolis*. Chicago: University of Chicago Press.

Lewis, R. (2017). Comments on urban agency: Relational space and intentionality. *Urban History* 44(1), 137–144.

Lewis, S. L. (2016). *Cities in Motion: Urban Life and Cosmopolitanism in Southeast Asia, 1920–1940*. Cambridge: Cambridge University Press.

Lila, M. (2019). The die-hard Raptors fan who embodies the best of Toronto (it's not Drake). *Globe and Mail,* May 29.

Lithwick, H. (1973). The problem with urban problems. In L. Axworthy and J. M. Gillies, eds, *The City: Canada's Prospects, Canada's Problems*. Toronto: Butterworth, pp. 20–25.

Little, B. R. (2014). *Me, Myself, and Us: The Science of Personality and the Art of Well-Being*. Toronto: HarperCollins.

Little, K. L. (1973). *African Women in Towns: An Aspect of Africa's Social Revolution*. Cambridge: Cambridge University Press.

Little, K. L. (1974). *Urbanisation As a Social Process: An Essay on Movement and Change in Contemporary Africa*. London: Routledge and Kegan Paul.

Lofland, L. H. (1989). Social life in the public realm: A review. *Journal of Contemporary Ethnography* 17(4), 453–482.

Lubove, R. (1962). *The Progressives and the Slums: Tenement House Reform in New York City, 1890–1917*. Pittsburgh: University of Pittsburgh Press.

Lucassen, L. (2013). Population and migration. In P. Clark, ed., *The Oxford Handbook of Cities in World History*. New York: Oxford University Press, pp. 664–682.

Luckin, B. (2000). Pollution in the city. In M. Daunton, ed., *The Cambridge History of Urban Britain, Vol. 3: 1840–1950*. Cambridge: Cambridge University Press, pp. 207–228.

Mabogunje, A. L., J. E. Hardoy, and R. P. Misra, eds. (1978). *Shelter Provision in Developing Countries: The Influence of Standards and Criteria*. New York: SCOPE.

Mace, R. (2008). Reproducing in cities. *Science* 319(5864), 764–765.

Mackintosh, P., R. Dennis, and D. W. Holdsworth, eds. (2018). *Architectures of Hurry: Mobilities, Cities and Modernity*. New York: Routledge.

Mandell, N. (2019). A hotel of her own: Building by and for the New Woman, 1900–1930. *Journal of Urban History* 45(3),517–541.

Marcus, S. (1999). *Apartment Stories: City and Home in Nineteenth Century Paris and London*. Berkeley, CA: University of California Press.

Marshall, A. (1922). *Principles of Economics: An Introductory Volume*, 8th ed. London: Macmillan.

Martindale, D. (1958). Prefatory remarks: The theory of the city. In M. Weber, *The City*. Glencoe, IL: The Free Press, pp. 9–62.

Mayne, A. (2017). *Slums: The History of a Global Injustice*. London: Reaktion.

McCann, L. (2017). *Imagining Uplands: John Olmsted's Masterpiece of Residential Design*. Victoria, BC: Brighton Press.

McCann, P. (2011). The role of industrial clustering and increasing returns to scale in economic development and urban growth. In N. Brooks, K. Donaghy, and G.-J. Knaap, eds, *The Oxford Handbook of Urban Economics and Planning*. New York: Oxford University Press, pp. 167–199.

McCormick, D. (1999). African enterprise clusters and industrialization: Theory and reality. *World Development* 27(9), 1531–1551.

McCormick, D. and B. Oyelaran-Oyeyinka, eds. (2007). *Industrial Clusters and Innovation Systems in Africa: Institutions, Markets and Policy*. Tokyo: United Nations University Press.

McCrossen, A. (2013). *Marking Modern Times: A History of Clocks, Watches and Other Timekeepers in American Life*. Chicago: University of Chicago Press.

McKelvey, B. (1963). *The Urbanization of America, 1860–1915*. New Brunswick, NJ: Rutgers University Press.

McKenzie, E. (2011). *Beyond Privatopia: Rethinking Residential Private Government*. Washington, DC: Urban Institute Press.

McShane, C. (2006). The state of the art in North American urban history. *Journal of Urban History* 32(4), 582–597.

Melosi, M. (2000). *The Sanitary City: Urban Infrastructure in America from Colonial Times to the Present*. Baltimore: Johns Hopkins University Press.

Melosi, M. (2013). The urban environment. In P. Clark, ed., *Cities in World History*. Oxford: Oxford University Press, pp. 700–719.

Melvin, P. M. (1987). *The Organic City: Urban Definition and Community Organization, 1880–1920*. Lexington: University of Kentucky Press.

Meyer, W. B. (2013). *Environmental Advantages of Cities: Countering Commonsense Anti-Urbanism*. Cambridge, MA: MIT Press.

Meyerowitz, J. J. (1988). *Women Adrift: Independent Wage Earners in Chicago, 1880–1930*. Chicago: University of Chicago Press.

Milgram, S. (1970). The experience of living in cities. *Science* 167(3924), 1461–1468.

Miner, H., ed. (1967). *The City in Modern Africa*. London: Pall Mall Press.

Mitchell, J. C. (1987). *Cities, Society and Social Perception: A Central African Perspective*. Oxford: Clarendon Press.

Mitullah, W. (2018). Urban governance: Transcending conventional urban governance. In D. Iossifora, C. N. H. Doll, and A. Gasparatos, eds, *Defining the Urban: Interdisciplinary and Professional Perspectives*. New York: Routledge, pp. 153–162.

Mohl, R. (1998). City and region: The missing dimension in U.S. urban history. *Journal of Urban History* 25(1), 3–22.

Mok, D., B. Wellman, and J. Carrasca. (2010). Does distance matter in the age of the internet? *Urban Studies* 47(13), 2747–2783.

Moller, V. (2020). *The Map of Knowledge: A Thousand-Year History of How Classical Ideas Were Lost and Found*. New York: Penguin Random House.

Molotch, H. (1976). The city as a growth machine: Toward a political economy of place. *American Journal of Sociology* 82(2), 309–332.

Monkkonen, E. H. (1988). *America Becomes Urban: The Development of U.S. Cities and Towns, 1780–1980*. Berkeley and Los Angeles: University of California Press.

Moreno-Monroy, A. (2012). Informality in space: Understanding agglomeration economies during economic development. *Urban Studies* 49(10), 2019–2030.

Morris, R. J. (1990). Externalities, the market, power structure and the urban agenda. *Urban History Yearbook* 17, 99–109.

Morris, R. J. (2000). Governance: Two centuries of urban growth. In R. J. Morris and R. H. Trainor, eds, *Urban Governance: Britain and Beyond Since 1750*. Aldershot: Ashgate, pp. 395–426.

Morris, R. N. (1968). *Urban Sociology*. London: Allen & Unwin.

Mosley, S. (2001). *The Chimney of the World: A History of Smoke Pollution in Victorian and Edwardian Manchester*. Cambridge: White Horse Press.

Mosley, S. (2010). *Environment in World History*. London: Routledge.

Moss, E. (2019). *Night Raiders: Burglary and the Making of Modern Urban Life in London 1860–1968*. New York: Oxford University Press.

Mumford, L. (1961). *The City in History*. London: Penguin.

Murphy, R. (1954). The city as a center of change: Western Europe and China. *Annals of the Association of American Geographers* 44(4), 349–362.

Narayana, M. R. (2011). Globalization and urban economic growth: Evidence for Bangalore, India. *International Journal of Urban and Regional Research* 35(6), 1284–1301.

Netflix (2020). *Cheer*. https://www.netflix.com/ca/title/81039393

Neumann, T. (2016). *Remaking the Rust Belt: The Postindustrial Transformation of North America*. Philadelphia: University of Pennsylvania Press.

Nieto, A. T. (2019). *Metropolitan Economic Development: The Political Economy of Urbanisation in Mexico*. New York: Routledge.

Nightingale, C. (2012). *Segregation: A Global History of Divided Cities*. Chicago: University of Chicago Press.

Nightingale, C. (2018). The Global Urban History Project. *Planning Perspectives* 33(1), 135–138.

Nissim, R. (2008). *Land Administration and Practice in Hong Kong*. Hong Kong: Hong Kong University Press.

Nye, D. E. (2018). *American Illumination: Urban Lighting 1800–1920*. Cambridge, MA: MIT Press.

Ogorzalek, T. (2018). *The Cities on the Hill: How Urban Institutions Transform National Politics*. Oxford: Oxford University Press.

Oliver, P., I. Davis, and I. Beverly. (1981). *Dunroamin: The Suburban Semi and Its Enemies*. London: Barrie and Jenkins.

Owen, D. (2009). *Green Metropolis*. New York: Penguin.

Pahl, R. E. (1968). The rural-urban continuum. In R. E. Pahl, ed., *Readings in Urban Sociology*. London: Pergamon, pp. 263–297.

Palmer, B. (2000). *Cultures of Darkness: Night Travels in the Histories of Transportation*. New York: Monthly Review Press.

Park, R. E. ([1929] 1967). The city as social laboratory. In R. H. Turner, ed., *Robert Park on Social Control and Collective Behavior*. Chicago: Phoenix, pp. 3–18.

Parker, S. (2004). *Urban Theory and the Urban Experience: Encountering the City*. New York: Routledge.

Parnell, S. (2016). Defining a global urban development agenda. *World Development* 78, 529–540.

Parnell, S. and J. Robinson. (2016). The global urban: Difference and complexity in urban studies and the science of cities. In S. Hall and R. Burdett, eds,

The Sage Handbook of the 21st Century City. Thousand Oaks, CA: Sage, pp. 13–31.

Parr, J. (1990). *The Gender of Breadwinners: Women, Men, and Change in Two Industrial Towns, 1880–1950*. Toronto: University of Toronto Press.

Peattie, L. (1994). An argument for slums. *Journal of Planning Education and Research*. 13(2), 136–143.

Peil, M. and P. Sada. (1984). *African Urban Society*. New York: Wiley.

Peiss, K. (1986). *Cheap Amusements: Working Women and Leisure in Turn-of-the-Century New York*. Philadelphia: Temple University Press.

Peterson, G. (2009). *Unlocking Land Values to Finance Urban Infrastructure*. Washington, DC: World Bank.

Peterson, J. (1983). The impact of sanitary reform upon American urban planning, 1840–1890. In D. A. Krueckeberg, ed., *Introduction to Planning History in the United States*. New Brunswick, NJ: Rutgers University Center for Urban Policy Research, pp. 13–19.

Phelps, N. and T. Ozawa. (2003). Contrasts in agglomeration: Proto-industrial, industrial and post-industrial forms compared. *Progress in Human Geography* 27(5), 583–604.

Pickvance, C. (1986). Comparative urban analysis and assumptions about causality. *International Journal of Urban and Regional Research* 10(2), 162–184.

Platt, H. (2005). *Shock Cities: The Environmental Transformation and Reform of Manchester and Chicago*. Chicago: University of Chicago Press.

Polèse, M. (2009). *The Wealth and Poverty of Regions: Why Cities Matter*. Chicago: University of Chicago Press.

Polèse, M. (2020). *The Wealth and Poverty and Cities: Why Nations Matter*. Oxford: Oxford University Press.

Portes, A. and W. Haller. (2005). The informal economy. In N. J. Smelser and R. Swedberg, eds, *The Handbook of Economic Sociology*. Princeton, NJ: Princeton University Press, pp. 403–425.

Potts, D. (2010). *Circular Migration in Zimbabwe and Contemporary Sub-Saharan Africa*. Oxford: James Currey.

Pred, A. (1973). The growth and development of systems of cities in advanced economies. In A. Pred and G. Tornquist, eds, *Systems of Cities and Information Flows*. Lund, Sweden: Gleerup, pp. 9–82.

Pred, A. (1980). *Urban Growth and City Systems in the United States, 1840–1860*. Cambridge, MA: Harvard University Press.

Prest, J. (1960). *The Industrial Revolution in Coventry*. London: Oxford University Press.

Prestel, J. B. (2017). *Emotional Cities: Debates on Urban Change in Berlin and Cairo, 1869–1910*. New York: Oxford University Press.

Putnam, R. D. (1993). *Making Democracy Work: Civic Traditions in Modern Italy*. Princeton, NJ: Princeton University Press.

Raban, J. (1973). *Soft City*. London: Hamish Hamilton.

Rae, D. (2003). *City: Urbanism and Its End*. New Haven, CT: Yale University Press.

Rast, J. (2012). Why history (still) matters: Time and temporality in urban political analysis. *Urban Affairs Review* 48(1), 3–36.

Reader, J. (2004). *Cities*. London: Heinemann.

Reeder, D. and R. Rodger. (2000). Industrialization and the city economy. In M. Daunton, ed., *The Cambridge Urban History of Britain, Vol. 3: 1840–1950*. Cambridge: Cambridge University Press, pp. 553–592.

Redfield, R. and M. Singer. ([1954] 1969). The cultural role of cities. In R. Sennett, ed., *Classic Essays on the Culture of Cities*. New York: Appleton-Century-Crofts, pp. 206–233.

Ren, X. (2018). Governing the informal: Housing policies over informal settlements in China, India and Brazil. *Housing Policy Debate* 28(1), 79–83.

Reuleche, J. (1984). The Ruhr: Centralization versus decentralization in a region of cities. In A. Sutcliffe, ed., *Metropolis 1890–1940*. London: Mansell, pp. 381–402.

Reuss, M. and S. Cutliffe, eds. (2010). *Illusory Boundary: Environment and Technology in History*. Charlottesville, VA: University of Virginia Press.

Robichaud, A. (2019). *Animal City: The Domestication of America*. Cambridge, MA: Harvard University Press.

Robinson, J. (1996). *Power of Apartheid: State, Power and Space in South African Cities*. Oxford: Butterworth-Heinemann.

Robinson, J. (2005). *Ordinary Cities: Between Modernity and Development*. London: Routledge.

Robinson, J. (2011). Cities in a world of cities: The comparative gesture. *International Journal of Urban and Regional Research* 35(1), 1–23.

Robson, B. T. (1973). *Urban Growth: An Approach*. London: Methuen.

Rodger, R. (1993). Theory, practice and European urban history. In R. Rodger, ed., *European Urban History. Prospect and Retrospect*. Leicester: Leicester University Press, pp. 1–18.

Rodger, R. (2003). Taking stock: Perspectives on British urban history. *Urban History Review* 32(1), 54–63.

Rodger, R. and R. Sweet (2008). *The Changing Nature of Urban History: History in Focus*. London: Institute of Historical Research, University of London.

Rodríguez-Pose, A. and R. Crescenzi. (2008). Mountains in a flat world: Why proximity still matters for the location of economic activity. *Cambridge Journal of Regions, Economy and Society* 1(3), 371–388.

Rodríguez-Pose, A. and R. Crescenzi. (2012). Do clusters generate greater innovation and growth? An analysis of European regions. *The Professional Geographer* 6(2), 211–231.

Rogaski, R. (2004). *Hygienic Modernity: Meanings of Health and Disease in Treaty-Port China.* Berkeley: University of California Press.

Rohe, W. M. (2009). From local to global: One hundred years of neighborhood planning. *Journal of the American Planning Association* 75(2), 209–230.

Rome, A. (2001). *The Bulldozer in the Countryside: Suburban Sprawl and the Rise of American Environmentalism.* Cambridge: Cambridge University Press.

Rosenthal, S. S. and Strange, W. C. (2004). Evidence on the nature and sources of agglomeration economies. In H. V. Henderson and J.-F. Thisse, eds, *Handbook of Regional and Urban Economics, Vol. 4: Cities and Geography.* Amsterdam: Elsevier, pp. 2119–2171.

Rossi, U. (2017). *Cities in Global Capitalism.* Cambridge: Polity.

Roweis, S. and A. J. Scott. (1978). The urban land question. In K. R. Cox, ed., *Urbanization and Conflict in Market Societies.* Chicago: Maaroufa, pp. 38–75.

Roy, A. (2005). Urban informality: Toward an epistemology of planning. *Journal of the American Planning Association* 71(2), 147–158.

Roy, A. (2015). Who's afraid of postcolonial theory? *International Journal of Urban and Regional Research* 40(1), 200–209.

Sandoval-Strausz, A. K. (2007). *Hotel: An American History.* New Haven, CT: Yale University Press.

Sandoval-Strausz, A. K. and N. Kwak, eds. (2018). *Making Cities Global: The Transnational Turn in Urban History.* Philadelphia: University of Pennsylvania Press.

Sassen, S. (2001). Cities in the global economy. In R. Paddison, ed., *Handbook of Urban Studies.* London: Sage, pp. 256–272.

Sassen, S. (2005). The global city: Introducing a concept. *Brown Journal of World Affairs* 11(2), 27–93.

Satyanath, S. (2018). Kokima language variation and change in a small but diverse city in India. In D. Smakman and P. Heinrich, eds, *Urban Sociolinguistics: The City As a Linguistic Process and Experience.* London: Routledge, pp. 95–112.

Saunders, D. (2010). *Arrival City: The Final Migration and the Next World.* Toronto: Knopf.

Saunders, P. (1981). *Social Theory and the Urban Question*. New York: holmes and Meier.

Saunders, P. (1985). Space, the city and urban sociology. In D. Gregory and J. Urry, eds, *Social Relations and Spatial Structures*. London: Methuen, pp. 67–89.

Saunier, P.-Y. (2013). *Transnational History*. Houndmills: Palgrave Macmillan.

Saunier, P.-Y. and S. Ewen. (2008). *Another Global City: Historical Explorations into the Transnational Municipal Moment, 1850–2000*. Basingstoke: Palgrave Macmillan.

Schaffer, D. (1988). *Two Centuries of American Planning*. Baltimore: Johns Hopkins University Press.

Schlesinger, A. M. (1933). *The Rise of the City 1878–1898*. New York: Macmillan.

Schlesinger, A. M. ([1949] 1973). The city in American civilization. In J. B. Callow, ed., *American Urban History: An Interpretative Reader with Commentaries*. New York: Oxford University Press, pp. 35–51.

Schott, D., Luckin, B., and G. Massard-Guilbaut, eds. (2005). *Resources of the City: Contributions to an Environmental History of Modern Europe*. Burlington, VT: Ashgate.

Schubert, D. (2000). The neighbourhood paradigm: From garden cities to gated communities. In R. Freestone, ed., *Urban Planning in a Changing World: The Twentieth Century Experience*. London: E and FN Spon, pp. 118–138.

Schultz, S. K. (1989). *Constructing Urban Culture: American Cities and City Planning, 1800–1920*. Philadelphia: Temple University Press.

Schultz, S. K. and C. McShane (1978). To engineer the metropolis: Sewers, sanitation, and city planning in late nineteenth-century America. *Journal of American History* 65(2), 389–411.

Schuyler, D. (1986). *The New Urban Landscape: The Redefinition of City Form in Nineteenth Century America*. Baltimore: Johns Hopkins University Press.

Scott, A. J. (1980). *The Urban Land Nexus and the State*. London: Pion.

Scott, A. J. (2000). *The Cultural Economy of Cities: Essays on the Geography of Image-Producing Industries*. New York: Sage.

Scott, A. J. (2006). Creative cities: Conceptual issues and policy questions. *Journal of Urban Affairs* 28(1), 1–17.

Scott, A. J. and M. Storper. (2015). The nature of cities: The scope and limits of urban theory. *International Journal of Urban and Regional Research* 39(1), 1–15.

Scott, P. (2000). The evolution of Britain's urban built environment. In M. Daunton, ed., *The Cambridge Urban History of Britain, Vol. 3: 1840–1950*. Cambridge: Cambridge University Press, pp. 495–523.

Sellers, J. (2003). Transnational urban associations and the state: Contemporary Europe compared with the Hanseatic League. In N. Ronderaad, ed., *Yearbook of European Administrative History* 15, 298–308.

Sennett, R. (1974). *The Fall of Public Man: On the Social Psychology of Capitalism*. New York: Random House.

Sewell, W. H. (2005). *Logics of History: Social Theory and Social Transformation*. Chicago: University of Chicago Press.

Shearmur, R. (2015). Far from the madding crowd: Slow innovators, information value, and the geography of innovation. *Growth and Change* 46(3), 424–442.

Shearmur, R, C. Carrincazeaux, and D. Doloreux, eds. (2016). *Handbook on the Geographies of Innovation*. London: Edward Elgar.

Sies, M. C. and C. Silver, eds. (1996). *Planning the Twentieth-Century American City*. Baltimore, MD: Johns Hopkins University Press.

Simmel, G. ([1903] 1969). The metropolis and mental life. In R. Sennett, ed., *Classic Essays in the Culture of Cities*. New York: Appleton-Century-Crofts, pp. 47–60.

Simmie, J. (2004). Innovation clusters and competitive cities in the UK and Europe. In M. Boddy and M. Parkinson, eds, *City Matters: Competitiveness, Cohesion and Urban Governance*. Bristol: Policy Press, pp. 171–198.

Sjoberg, G. (1960). *The Pre-Industrial City*. New York: Free Press.

Smakman, D. and P. Heinrich, eds. (2018). *Urban Sociolinguistics: The City As a Linguistic Process and Experience*. London: Routledge.

Smith, A. ([1776] 1970). *The Wealth of Nations*. Harmondsworth: Penguin.

Smith, M. P. and J. Eade, eds. (2008). *Transnational Ties: Cities, Migrations, and Identities*. New Brunswick, NJ: Transaction Publishers.

Spain, D. (2014). Gender and urban space. *Annual Review of Sociology* 40: 581–598.

Stanger-Ross, J. (2009). *Staying Italian: Urban Change and Ethnic Life in Postwar Toronto and Philadelphia*. Chicago: University of Chicago Press.

Stapleton, K. (2016). In search of frameworks for productive comparison of cities in world history. *Journal of Modern Chinese History* 10(2), 230–247.

Stave, B., ed. (1981). *Modern Industrial Cities: History, Policy, and Survival*. Beverley Hills: Sage.

Stave, B. (1983). In pursuit of urban history: Conversations with myself and others – a view from the United States. In D. Fraser and A. Sutcliffe, eds, *The Pursuit of Urban History*. London: Arnold, pp. 407–427.

Stebley, N. M. (1987). Helping behavior in rural and urban environments: A meta analysis. *Psychological Bulletin* 102(3), 346–356.

Stedman Jones, G. (1971). *Outcast London: A Study in the Relationship Between Classes in Victorian Society*. Oxford: Oxford University Press.

Stelter, G. A. (1977). A sense of time and place: The historian's approach to Canada's urban past. In G. A. Stelter and A. F. J. Artibise, eds, *The Canadian City*. Toronto: McClelland and Stewart, pp. 420–441.

Stevenson, D. (2003). *Cities and Urban Cultures*. Maidenhead: Open University Press.

Stinchcombe, A. L. (1968). *Constructing Social Theories*. New York: Harcourt, Brace and World.

Stone, L. (1977). History and the social sciences in the twentieth century. In C. E. Delzell, ed., *The Future of History: Essays in the Vanderbilt University Centennial Symposium*. Nashville, TN: Vanderbilt University Press, pp. 3–42.

Storper, M. (1995). The resurgence of regions ten years later: The region as a nexus of untraded interdependencies. *European Urban and Regional Studies* 2(3), 191–221.

Storper, M. (2013). *Keys to the City: How Economics, Institutions, Social Interactions, and politics Shape Development*. Princeton, NJ: Princeton University Press.

Storper, M. and A. J. Venables. (2004). Buzz: Face-to-face contact and the urban economy. *Journal of Economic Geography* 4(4), 351–370.

Strange, C. (1995). *Toronto's Girl Problem: The Perils and Pleasures of the City, 1880–1930*. Toronto: University of Toronto Press.

Sugrue, T. (1996). *The Origins of the Urban Crisis: Race and Inequality in Postwar Detroit*. Princeton, NJ: Princeton University Press.

Sutcliffe, A., ed. (1974). *Multi-Storey Living: The British Working-Class Experience*. London: Croom Helm.

Sutcliffe, A. (1981). *Towards the Planned City: Germany, Britain, the United States, and France, 1780–1914*. New York: St. Martin's Press.

Szreter, S. and A. Hardy. (2000). Urban fertility and mortality patterns. In M. Daunton, ed., *The Cambridge Urban History of Britain, Vol. 2: 1840–1950*. Cambridge: Cambridge University Press, pp. 629–672.

Tarr, J. A. (1996). *The Search for the Ultimate Sink: Urban Pollution in Historical Perspective*. Akron: University of Akron Press.

Taylor, P. J. and B. Derudder. (2016). *World City Network: A Global Urban Analysis*. London: Routledge.

Taylor, Z. (2014). If different, then why? Explaining the divergent political development of Canadian and American local governance. *International Journal of Canadian Studies* 49(1), 53–79.

Teaford, J. (1984). *The Unheralded Triumph: City Government in America 1870–1900*. Baltimore, MD: Johns Hopkins University Press.

Teaford, J. (2006). *The Metropolitan Revolution: The Rise of Post-urban America*. New York: Columbia University Press.

Thernstrom, S. (1973). Reflections on the new urban history. In A. B. Callow, ed., *American Urban History: An Interpretative Reader with Commentaries*. New York: Oxford University Press, pp. 672–684.

Tilly, C. (1984). *Big Structures, Large Processes, Huge Comparisons*. New York: Russell Sage.

Tilly, C. (1996). What good is urban history? *Journal of Urban History* 22(6), 709–719.

Tolbert, L. (2017). Henry, a slave, v. State of Tennessee: The public and private space of slaves in a small town. In C. Ellis and R. Ginsburg, eds, *Slavery in the City. Architecture and Landscapes of Urban Slavery in North America*. Charlottesville: University of Virginia Press, pp. 140–152.

Turner, R. E. ([1940] 1973). The industrial city: Center of cultural change. In A. B. Callow, ed., *American Urban History: An Interpretative Reader with Commentaries*. New York: Oxford University Press, pp. 180–189.

UN Habitat (2013). *State of the World's Cities 2012/13: Prosperity of Cities*. London: Earthscan.

Valverde, M. (1991). *The Age of Light, Soap and Water: Moral Reform in English Canada, 1885–1925*. Toronto: McClelland and Stewart.

Valverde, M. (2011). Seeing like a city: The dialectic of modern and premodern ways of seeing in urban governance. *Law and Society Review* 45(2), 277–312.

Vance, J. (1967). Housing the worker: Determinative and contingent ties in nineteenth century Birmingham. *Economic Geography* 43(2), 95–127.

Vanderbilt, T. (2008). *Traffic*. New York: Knopf.

Vaughan, L. (2018). *Mapping Society: The Spatial Dimensions of Social Cartography*. London: University College London Press.

Visser, R. (2010). *Cities Surround the Countryside: Urban Aesthetics in Postsocialist China*. Durham, NC: Duke University Press.

Vlach, J. M. (1997). "Without recourse to owners": The architecture of urban slavery in the Antebellum South. In C. L. Hudgins and E. C. Cromley, eds, *Perspectives in Vernacular Architecture, Vol. 6: Shaping Communities*. Knoxville, TN: University of Tennessee Press, pp. 150–160.

Von Hoffman, A. (1994). *Local Attachments: The Making of an American Neighborhood*. Baltimore, MD: Johns Hopkins University Press.

Wade, R. (1959). *The Urban Frontier: Pioneer Life in Early Pittsburgh, Cincinnati, Lexington, Louisville, and St. Louis*. Chicago: University of Chicago Press.

Wade, R. (1964). *Slavery in the Cities: The South, 1820–1860*. New York: Oxford University Press.

Walton, J. and L. H. Masotti, eds. (1976). *The City in Comparative Perspective: Cross-National Research and New Directions in Theory.* New York: Halsted Press.

Ward, D. (1989). *Poverty, Ethnicity and the American City, 1840–1925: Changing Conceptions of the Slum and the Ghetto.* Cambridge: Cambridge University Press.

Ward, D. (1990). Social reform, social surveys and the discovery of the modern city. *Annals of the Association of American Geographers* 80(4), 491–503.

Ward, K. (2008). Towards a comparative (re)turn in urban studies? Some reflections. *Urban Geography* 27(5), 405–410.

Ward, S. V. (2000). Re-examining the international diffusion of planning. In R. Freestone, ed., *Urban Planning in a Changing World.* London: E and FN Spon, pp. 40–60.

Warner, S. A. (1962). *Streetcar Suburbs: The Process of Growth in Boston, 1870–1900.* Cambridge, MA: Harvard University Press.

Warner, S. B. (1968). If all the world were Philadelphia: A scaffolding for urban history, 1774–1930. *American Historical Review* 74(1), 26–43.

Warner, S. B. (1991). When urban history is at the centre of the curriculum. *Journal of Urban History* 18, 3–9.

Webber, M. M. (1964). The urban place and the nonplace urban realm. In M. M. Webber, ed., *Explorations into Urban Structure.* Philadelphia: University of Pennsylvania Press, pp. 79–153.

Weber, A. ([1899] 1963). *The Growth of Cities in the Nineteenth Century: A Study in Statistics.* Ithaca, NY: Cornell University Press.

Weigel, M. (2016). *Labor of Love: The Invention of Dating.* New York: Farrar, Straus and Giroux.

Weiss, M. (1987). *The Rise of the Community Builders: The American Real Estate Industry and Urban Land Planning.* New York: Columbia University Press.

Wertheim, W. F. (1964). *Indonesian Society in Transition: A Study in Social Change.* The Hague: W. van Hoeve.

Wessel, T. (2009). Does diversity in urban space enhance intergroup contact and tolerance? *Geografiska Annaler Series B. Human Geography* 91B(1), 5–17.

Wheatley, P. (2001). *The Places Where Men Pray Together: Cities in Islamic Lands, Seventh through the Tenth Centuries.* Chicago: University of Chicago Press.

White, M. and L. White. (1962). *The Intellectual Versus the City.* Cambridge, MA: Harvard University Press.

Williams, R. (1975). *The Country and the City.* St. Albans: Paladin.

Winder, G. (1999). The North American manufacturing belt in 1880: A cluster of regional industrial systems or one large industrial district? *Economic Geography* 75(1), 71–92.

Wirth, L. ([1938] 1969). Urbanism as a way of life. In R. Sennett, ed., *Classic Essays on the Culture of Cities*. New York: Appleton-Century-Crofts, pp. 143–164.

Wirth, L. ([1956] 1969). Rural-urban differences. In R. Sennett, ed., *Classic Essays on the Culture of Cities*. New York: Appleton-Century-Crofts, pp. 165–169.

Wolfe, D. A. and M. S. Gertler, eds. (2016). *Growing Urban Economies: Innovation, Creativity and Governance in Canadian City-Regions*. Toronto: University of Toronto Press.

Wrigley, E. A. (1967). A simple model of London's importance in changing English society and economy 1650–1750. *Past and Present* 37(1), 44–70.

Wu, W. and P. Gaubatz. (2013). *The Chinese City*. New York: Routledge.

Yanarella, E. J. (2011). *City As Fulcrum of Global Sustainability*. London: Anthem.

Yates, A. (2015). *Selling Paris: Property and Commercial Culture in the Fin-de -Siècle Capital*. Cambridge, MA: Harvard University Press.

Yelling, J. A. (2000). Land, property and planning. In M. Daunton, ed., *The Cambridge Urban History of Britain, Vol. 3: 1840–1950*. Cambridge: Cambridge University Press, pp. 467–494.

Yeoh, B. (1996). *Contesting Space: Power Relations and the Urban Built Environment in Colonial Singapore*. Oxford: Oxford University Press.

Young, L. (2013). *Beyond the Metropolis: Second Cities and Modern Life in Japan*. Berkeley: University of California Press.

Zukin, S. (1995). *The Cultures of Cities*. Cambridge, MA: Blackwell.

Zunz, O. (1982). *The Changing Face of Inequality: Urbanization, Industrial Development and Immigrants in Detroit, 1880–1920*. Chicago: University of Chicago Press.

Acknowledgments

Ever since I began to describe my research interests as 'urban' – and that is a long time ago – I have been conscious of the need to explain to myself exactly what that means. From time to time, in a half-hearted sort of way, I've tried to do that, but never wholeheartedly, and for most of the time I have been content to let the question slide. That is why I was delighted when the editors of this new series offered me the opportunity to assemble fragmentary thoughts into what I hope is a meaningful and coherent whole.

I need to explain the other element of the identity that I present here: honorary historian. I was trained as a geographer, but a high school teacher (Mr Ganderton), my director of studies at Cambridge (Jack Langton), Peter Goheen at Queen's, and then the first Canadian urban history conference in Guelph, Ontario in 1977, gently drew me in. For my PhD, I studied the 1960s and structured the dissertation thematically, but when I came to write the book that developed out of my thesis somehow the material organized itself as a narrative. I found myself on a new path. I embraced 'historical geographer' as a respectable hybrid identity but found the unmissable conferences to be those of urban and planning historians. That is why here, when speaking about or to urban historians, I use 'we', not 'they'. I hope no one finds this presumptuous or disloyal.

The long list of references reveals my multiple intellectual debts, but let me single out those who have contributed most directly to the arguments articulated here, including one anonymous reviewer and another who revealed their identity. I would especially like to thank the following writers for their thoughtful and helpful comments on a draft of all or part of this Element, or for especially valuable input over the years: Bob Beauregard, Harold Bérubé, Bob Brenner, Kevin Cox, Richard Dennis, Peter Goheen, Robert Lewis, Jeff Lin, Carl Nightingale, Mario Polèse, Jenny Robinson, Richard Rodger, Michael Smith, Kristin Stapleton, and Richard Walker. It should go without saying that all would disagree at some point with what I have written. I would like to dedicate this Element to Peter Goheen, for getting the whole thing going.

Cambridge Elements ⁼

Global Urban History

Series Editors

Michael Goebel
Graduate Institute Geneva

Michael Goebel is the Pierre du Bois Chair Europe and the World and Associate Professor of International History at the Graduate Institute Geneva. His research focuses on the histories of nationalism, of cities, and of migration. He is the author of Anti-Imperial Metropolis: Interwar Paris and the Seeds of Third World Nationalism (2015).

Tracy Neumann
Wayne State University

Tracy Neumann is an Associate Professor of History at Wayne State University. Her research focuses on global and transnational approaches to cities and the built environment. She is the author of Remaking the Rust Belt: The Postindustrial Transformation of North America (2016) and of essays on urban history and public policy.

Joseph Ben Prestel
Freie Universität Berlin

Joseph Ben Prestel is an Assistant Professor (wissenschaftlicher Mitarbeiter) of history at Freie Universität Berlin. His research focuses on the histories of Europe and the Middle East in the nineteenth and twentieth centuries as well as on global and urban history. He is the author of Emotional Cities: Debates on Urban Change in Berlin and Cairo, 1860–1910 (2017).

About the Series

This series proposes a new understanding of urban history by reinterpreting the history of the world's cities. Emphasizing global, comparative, and transnational approaches, individual titles deliver empirical research about specific cities while also exploring questions that expand the narrative outside the immediate locale to give insights into global trends and conceptual debates.

Cambridge Elements ☰

Global Urban History

Elements in the Series

How Cities Matter
Richard Harris

Real Estate and Global Urban History
Alexia Yates

A full series listing is available at: www.cambridge.org/EGUB

Printed in the United States
by Baker & Taylor Publisher Services